Fun Facts About the RNC

From 1856 to 2020

Ernest Ducran

5

Table of Contents

Introduction

The roar of the crowd, the waving banners, the carefully crafted speeches – the Republican National Convention (RNC) is more than just a political gathering. It is a microcosm of American history itself, reflecting the nation's triumphs, struggles, and evolving identity. Behind the spectacle, beyond the soundbites, lie stories of ambition, strategy, and the constant push and pull of competing visions for the future of the United States. This book, "Fun Facts About the Republican National Conventions," delves into the hidden corners of this quadrennial event, unearthing fascinating anecdotes, forgotten controversies, and the often-overlooked impact of the RNC on the very fabric of American society.

From the smoke-filled rooms where backroom deals were struck to the podium where history-making speeches echoed, we will journey through each election year, starting with the first Republican National Convention in 1856. We will explore the unique character of each hosting city, understanding how its social fabric, economic landscape, and political leanings shaped the events that unfolded within convention halls. Philadelphia, Chicago, New York – these cities, and many others, served as stages for the drama of American democracy, their streets echoing with the hopes and anxieties of a nation on the cusp of change.

Each chapter will delve into the historical context surrounding each convention, offering a glimpse into the predominant issues of the day. Was it the specter of slavery that loomed large, or the anxieties of a world war? Was it economic hardship that fueled the national conversation, or the call for social justice? By understanding the challenges and aspirations of the time, we can better grasp the motivations of the key players – the presidents, the nominees, the party bosses, and the delegates – who shaped the course of the Republican Party and, in turn, the nation.

This book is not merely a dry recitation of dates and facts. It is a tapestry woven from the threads of personal ambition, political maneuvering, and unexpected twists of fate. We will uncover stories of unexpected victories and crushing defeats, of powerful alliances forged and bitter rivalries ignited. We will delve into the captivating speeches that stirred the souls of a nation, the strategic missteps that shifted the political landscape, and the unforeseen events that forever altered the trajectory of American history.

Did you know that the first Republican National Convention was convened to nominate a candidate to challenge the expansion of slavery? Or that a split within the party in 1912 paved the way for Woodrow Wilson's victory? Did you know that the 1964 convention witnessed a clash between moderate and conservative factions that continues to resonate within the party today? These are just a few of the many captivating narratives that await you within these pages.

More than just a collection of intriguing anecdotes, this book aims to highlight the lasting impact of the

Republican National Convention on the evolution of the United States. From shaping national policies to influencing social movements, from propelling technological advancements to navigating international relations, the decisions made and the platforms adopted at these conventions reverberated far beyond the convention hall.

By understanding the history of the RNC, we gain a deeper understanding of the complexities of the American political system. We witness the evolution of political discourse, the ebb and flow of ideological trends, and the enduring power of ideas. This book serves as a reminder that history is not a static entity, but rather a dynamic force that continues to shape the present and influence the future.

So, whether you are a history buff, a political junkie, or simply curious about the inner workings of American democracy, this book offers a unique and insightful look into the often-overlooked world of the Republican National Convention. Join us as we embark on this journey through time, unearthing the hidden stories, exploring the forgotten controversies, and revealing the enduring legacy of this pivotal event in American history.

1856: A Party Forged in the Fires of Freedom

Philadelphia. The City of Brotherly Love. Birthplace of the Declaration of Independence. In June of 1856, it became the cradle of the Republican Party, hosting the first ever Republican National Convention. This wasn't just another political gathering; it was a crucible, forging a new political force from the fires of fervent opposition to the expansion of slavery.

A Nation Divided

The year 1856 saw the United States teetering precariously on the brink of civil war. The issue of slavery, long a festering wound on the nation's conscience, had reached a critical point. The Kansas-Nebraska Act of 1854, which allowed for the potential expansion of slavery into new territories, had ignited a firestorm of controversy. Violent clashes between pro-slavery and anti-slavery factions erupted in Kansas, earning it the grim moniker "Bleeding Kansas."

The existing political landscape, dominated by the Whig and Democratic parties, seemed incapable of containing the escalating crisis. The Whigs, fractured by internal divisions over slavery, were on the verge of collapse.

The Democrats, though still a powerful force, were increasingly beholden to their pro-slavery Southern wing.

A New Hope: The Rise of the Republicans

It was in this turbulent atmosphere that the Republican Party emerged. Born from a coalition of anti-slavery Democrats, Whigs, and Free-Soilers, the Republicans represented a powerful new force in American politics. United by their unwavering opposition to the expansion of slavery, they also advocated for a platform of economic modernization, including support for railroads and internal improvements.

Leading figures in the burgeoning party included men like:

- **Horace Greeley:** The influential editor of the New York Tribune, Greeley's powerful editorials provided an important platform for anti-slavery views and helped popularize the Republican Party.
- **Salmon P. Chase:** A former Democrat and Senator from Ohio, Chase was a staunch abolitionist and a key figure in drafting the Republican platform.
- **William H. Seward:** The Senator from New York, Seward was a gifted orator and a rising star in the anti-slavery movement. His "irrepressible conflict" speech, delivered a year earlier, had become a rallying cry for opponents of slavery.

These men, along with many others, understood the urgency of the situation. The future of the nation, they believed, hung in the balance.

The First Republican National Convention

The convention itself was a spectacle that captured the nation's attention. Held in Philadelphia's Musical Fund Hall from June 17th to 19th, the gathering drew delegates from across the North and even a few brave souls from the slaveholding border states. The atmosphere inside the hall was electric, filled with a sense of purpose and anticipation.

The key tasks before the convention were to formally establish the party platform and nominate their candidates for President and Vice President.

The platform adopted at the convention was a bold and uncompromising document. It declared that slavery was a "relic of barbarism" and that its further expansion should be prohibited in all territories. This stance placed the Republicans in direct opposition to the dominant pro-slavery faction of the Democratic Party.

Frémont and Dayton: The First Standard Bearers

When it came to choosing their standard-bearer, the Republicans opted for a candidate who embodied the spirit of the frontier and westward expansion: **John C. Frémont**. A national hero known as "The Pathfinder" for his explorations of the American West, Frémont had no prior political experience. However, his stance against the expansion of slavery and his image as a

15

vigorous, independent leader resonated with the Republican base.

For Vice President, the convention selected **William L. Dayton**, a former Senator from New Jersey, known for his strong anti-slavery views and his experience in government.

A Defining Moment

The 1856 Republican National Convention was much more than just a political event. It was a defining moment in American history. The formation of the Republican Party and its unwavering stance against the expansion of slavery altered the political landscape forever. Though Frémont lost the 1856 election to Democrat James Buchanan, the Republicans proved to be a formidable force, garnering significant support in the North.

The seeds sown in that Philadelphia hall in June of 1856 would eventually blossom into a powerful movement that would guide the nation through the tumultuous years of Civil War and Reconstruction. The Republican Party, forged in the fires of the slavery debate, would go on to become one of the two dominant political parties in the United States, leaving an indelible mark on the nation's history.

1860: A House Divided and a Convention on the Brink

The year 1860 dawned with a palpable sense of dread across the United States. The issue of slavery, a festering wound on the nation's soul, had pushed North and South to the precipice of war. This precarious backdrop formed the dramatic setting for the 1860 Republican National Convention, held in Chicago, Illinois, a bustling city symbolizing the rapidly expanding West.

A City of Opportunity and the Rising Tide of Sectionalism

Chicago, with its strategic location on Lake Michigan and its burgeoning industries, embodied the dynamism and ambition of the young nation. Yet, even in this hub of progress, the shadow of slavery loomed large. The city was deeply divided, reflecting the larger national tension. While many Chicagoans sympathized with the abolitionist cause, the city also held a significant pro-slavery contingent, highlighting the complex realities of a nation on the brink of collapse.

The Republican Party, a mere six years old, was itself a product of this growing sectionalism. Formed in opposition to the expansion of slavery into new territories, the party drew together a diverse coalition of abolitionists, former Whigs, and anti-slavery Democrats. As the nation teetered on the edge, the Republicans recognized the urgency of their mission: to nominate a candidate capable of uniting the North and challenging the entrenched power of the pro-slavery South.

The Leaders and the Issues: A Nation at a Crossroads

The 1860 Republican National Convention saw a convergence of some of the most influential figures in American history. William H. Seward, the eloquent senator from New York, was considered the frontrunner. Salmon P. Chase, the staunchly anti-slavery governor of Ohio, presented a formidable challenge. Other notable contenders included Missouri's Edward Bates, known for his moderate stance, and the relatively unknown but charismatic Abraham Lincoln of Illinois.

The convention, held in Chicago's newly constructed Wigwam, a massive wooden structure built specifically for the event, pulsated with anticipation and political maneuvering. The central issue, naturally, was slavery. While the Republican platform condemned its expansion, there were deep divisions over how far to push the issue. Moderates favored containment, while radicals demanded outright abolition. Other key issues included tariffs, internal improvements, and the future of the West.

The Rise of Lincoln: A Dark Horse Triumphs

The nomination process was a tense affair, marked by backroom deals and impassioned speeches. Seward, initially considered the inevitable choice, faced resistance due to his perceived radicalism and his history of political maneuvering. Chase, though admired for his principles, lacked widespread appeal.

Enter Abraham Lincoln. Though less experienced than his rivals, Lincoln possessed a keen intellect, a calm demeanor, and a remarkable ability to connect with ordinary Americans. His famous "House Divided" speech, delivered the previous year, had established him as a powerful voice against the expansion of slavery.

Through a combination of shrewd political maneuvering by his supporters and his own growing reputation, Lincoln secured the nomination on the third ballot. The choice of Hannibal Hamlin, a former Democrat from Maine, as his running mate further demonstrated the party's commitment to unifying the North.

The Legacy of 1860: A Nation Forged in Crisis

The 1860 Republican National Convention was more than a political gathering; it was a pivotal moment in American history. The nomination of Lincoln, a man who embodied both the ideals and the anxieties of his time, proved to be a turning point.

Lincoln's victory in the general election, made possible by the fragmentation of the Democratic Party, pushed the already divided nation into the abyss of civil war. Yet, it was through this crucible of fire that the nation would ultimately confront its original sin and begin the long and arduous journey towards fulfilling its promise of liberty and equality for all.

The convention in Chicago, though seemingly insignificant compared to the tumultuous events that followed, laid the groundwork for a new era in American politics. It marked the emergence of the Republican Party as a major political force, one that would shape the destiny of the nation for generations to come. And, most importantly, it placed Abraham Lincoln, a man of unwavering principle and profound humanity, at the helm of a nation in peril, forever etching his name into the annals of history.

1864: A Convention Forged in Fire

The year is 1864. The very soul of a nation hangs precariously in the balance. The deafening roar of cannons echoes across a divided land, a constant reminder of the brutal Civil War that has gripped the nation for three long years. In this atmosphere thick with uncertainty and sorrow, the Republican Party, still in its relative infancy, gears up for its National Convention, held in Baltimore, Maryland, from June 7th to 8th.

A City on Edge, A Nation Divided

Choosing Baltimore as the host city was no accident. A bustling port city with divided loyalties, it served as a microcosm of the nation itself. Maryland, a slave state, had remained part of the Union, but only barely. Its streets had witnessed bloodshed during the Pratt Street Riot just three years prior, a stark reminder of the fragility of peace. Holding the convention in Baltimore was a strategic gamble, a bold statement of the Republicans' commitment to preserving the Union, even within a hotbed of conflicting ideologies.

War and Emancipation: Defining Issues of a Generation

The dominant issues of the 1864 convention were inescapably intertwined with the ongoing war. The very survival of the Union was at stake, and the question of slavery, long a festering wound on the nation's conscience, had taken center stage. The Emancipation Proclamation, issued by President Abraham Lincoln the year before, had fundamentally altered the conflict, transforming it from a fight to preserve the Union into a crusade for human freedom.

Titans of a Turbulent Time

The Republican Party of 1864 was a party of fervent abolitionists, pragmatic moderates, and war-weary citizens united by a single, powerful goal: to save the Union. Abraham Lincoln, the brooding, introspective lawyer from Illinois, led the party and the nation. His unwavering commitment to the Union, coupled with his eloquence and compassion, had made him a symbol of hope in a time of profound darkness.

Alongside Lincoln stood other towering figures of the era. William H. Seward, Lincoln's Secretary of State, a master strategist and shrewd diplomat, played a crucial role in keeping European powers out of the conflict. Edwin M. Stanton, the fiercely efficient Secretary of War, worked tirelessly to equip and supply the Union Army. Salmon P. Chase, former Secretary of the Treasury and a staunch abolitionist, harbored presidential aspirations, representing a faction of the party that considered Lincoln too moderate.

"Don't Swap Horses Midstream": The Re-Nomination of Lincoln

Despite his growing stature, Lincoln was not assured of his party's nomination. The war had taken a heavy toll, and some within the Republican ranks questioned his leadership. The Radical Republicans, a faction pushing for swift and uncompromising abolition, viewed Lincoln as too hesitant on the issue of slavery. They found a voice in John C. Frémont, the famed explorer and former presidential candidate, who initially challenged Lincoln for the nomination.

However, the convention ultimately rallied around Lincoln. His unwavering commitment to victory, coupled with the slogan "Don't swap horses midstream," resonated with a nation yearning for stability. The convention nominated Lincoln for a second term, choosing Andrew Johnson, a Southern Democrat loyal to the Union, as his running mate – a calculated move to broaden their appeal in the war-torn South.

A Platform Built on Unity and Freedom

The 1864 Republican platform was a testament to the party's evolution. Gone were the days of focusing solely on preventing the expansion of slavery. The platform now called for the complete abolition of slavery, enshrined in the Constitution as the 13th Amendment. This bold stance solidified the Republican Party's commitment to equality and justice for all, regardless of race.

Echoes of 1864: A Legacy Forged in Crisis

The 1864 Republican National Convention was more than a political gathering; it was a pivotal moment in American history. Held at a time when the nation teetered on the brink of collapse, it reaffirmed the principles of unity, freedom, and democracy. The convention's nomination of Lincoln, a man who embodied these ideals, and its adoption of a platform dedicated to ending slavery, set the stage for the final push towards Union victory and the long and arduous journey toward healing a wounded nation.

The echoes of 1864 remind us that even in the darkest of times, when hope seems lost and the future uncertain, courage, conviction, and an unwavering belief in the promise of a better tomorrow can guide a nation toward its highest aspirations.

1868: Chicago and the Rise of Grant

The year is 1868. The wounds of the Civil War, though slowly beginning to heal, still ran deep across the nation. Reconstruction dominated the political landscape, a complex and contentious process that pitted President Andrew Johnson against the Radical Republicans in Congress. In this tumultuous atmosphere, the Republican Party gathered in Chicago, a city rapidly rising from the ashes of a devastating fire just a year prior, to chart their course for the upcoming presidential election.

A City Reborn, A Nation Divided

Chicago, despite the recent devastation, pulsated with energy. Its selection as the host city for the Republican National Convention was no accident. It represented the burgeoning industrial heartland of the nation, a stark contrast to the war-torn South and a powerful symbol of Union strength and resilience. The city, eager to prove its recovery and national importance, welcomed the convention with open arms, draping its streets in patriotic bunting and erecting a massive temporary structure, the Wigwam, to house the thousands of delegates and spectators expected.

The Issues: Reconstruction and its Discontents

The shadow of the Civil War loomed large over the 1868 Republican National Convention. Reconstruction, the process of reintegrating the defeated Confederate states into the Union, dominated the political discourse. The Republican Party found itself deeply divided. On one side stood the moderate Republicans, led by President Johnson, who favored a lenient approach towards the former Confederate states. On the other, the Radical Republicans, spearheaded by figures like Thaddeus Stevens and Charles Sumner, pushed for a more stringent reconstruction process, one that ensured civil rights for freedmen and held the former Confederacy accountable for the war.

This internal struggle, played out against a backdrop of racial violence and political maneuvering in the South, created a sense of urgency at the convention. The delegates knew the future of the nation, and the fate of the newly emancipated African Americans, hung in the balance.

The Hero Emerges: Ulysses S. Grant

Amidst this volatile political landscape, one figure stood out as a beacon of unity and hope: Ulysses S. Grant. The former General of the Union Army, hailed as the hero of Appomattox, remained largely silent on political matters after the war. Yet, his unwavering commitment to the Union and his reputation for integrity and competence made him an immensely popular figure. Both moderate and Radical Republicans saw in Grant a potential unifier, a leader who could bridge the deep divisions within the party and the nation.

The Nomination and the Platform

The convention proceedings were not without their moments of tension. The platform committee witnessed fierce debates over the issue of Reconstruction. Eventually, a compromise was reached, advocating for a balance between leniency and accountability for the South, while firmly supporting the principles of equal rights for all citizens, regardless of race.

When it came time to choose their nominee, the Republicans turned to Grant. His nomination was met with thunderous applause, a testament to his widespread popularity and the party's belief in his ability to lead the nation through the turbulent waters of Reconstruction. Speaker after speaker extolled Grant's virtues, highlighting his wartime leadership, his unwavering commitment to the Union, and his reputation for honesty and integrity.

The Legacy of 1868

The 1868 Republican National Convention marked a pivotal moment in American history. The nomination of Grant, a war hero who transcended partisan divides, provided a sense of unity and hope in a nation still grappling with the wounds of war. The party platform, though a compromise, signaled a commitment to Reconstruction and the protection of Black civil rights.

The convention, held in a city still rebuilding from disaster, symbolized the resilience of the nation and the

Republican Party's commitment to progress and unity. It set the stage for Grant's victory in the general election and the continuation of Reconstruction, a period marked by both progress and setbacks in the fight for racial equality. The story of the 1868 Republican National Convention is ultimately a story of a nation in transition, searching for its place in a post-Civil War world, and placing its trust in a leader who embodied both its pain and its hope for the future.

1872: A Convention Amidst Scandal and Strife

Philadelphia, the City of Brotherly Love, was no stranger to pivotal moments in American history. It was here that the Declaration of Independence was signed, solidifying a break from British rule. It was here that the Constitution was framed, laying the foundation for a new nation. And in June of 1872, it was here that the Republican Party, still grappling with the legacy of the Civil War and the challenges of Reconstruction, gathered for its sixth national convention.

A Nation in Transition

The shadow of the Civil War loomed large in 1872. The nation was still reeling from the assassination of President Abraham Lincoln just seven years prior, and the wounds of conflict remained raw. Reconstruction, the ambitious project of rebuilding the South and integrating freed slaves into society, was proving to be a complex and contentious endeavor. Southern states, resistant to federal intervention and the expansion of Black rights, witnessed the rise of white supremacist groups like the Ku Klux Klan.

Amidst this turmoil, Ulysses S. Grant, the celebrated Civil War general, was concluding his first term as President. Grant, though a war hero, faced mounting criticism. His administration was plagued by scandals, tarnishing the Republican Party's reputation. The Crédit Mobilier scandal, which implicated members of Congress in a scheme to defraud the government, shook public trust.

Divisions Within the Ranks

The Republican Party of 1872 was not the unified force it had been during the war. Disillusioned by corruption and the slow pace of Reconstruction, a faction of Liberal Republicans emerged. This group, advocating for civil service reform and an end to Reconstruction policies they deemed excessive, challenged Grant's bid for re-election. They nominated Horace Greeley, a prominent newspaper editor and former Grant supporter, as their presidential candidate.

The Convention Unfolds

The Republican National Convention convened in Philadelphia's Academy of Music on June 5th, 1872. The atmosphere was charged with tension, reflecting the divisions within the party and the nation. Despite the challenges, Grant remained a popular figure, particularly among Black voters who saw him as their protector.

The convention itself was a tightly controlled affair. The platform, reaffirming support for Reconstruction and endorsing Grant's administration, was adopted with little debate. The nomination process was a mere formality. Grant was renominated by acclamation, solidifying his position as the party's standard-bearer. Senator Henry Wilson of Massachusetts, known for his staunch abolitionist views, was chosen as his running mate.

Beyond the Ballots

The 1872 Republican National Convention, while seemingly predictable, provides a window into a tumultuous period in American history. It showcases the challenges of governing a nation healing from war and grappling with deep social and political divisions.

The convention also highlights the evolving nature of the Republican Party. While the party of Lincoln had been forged in the fires of anti-slavery sentiment, it was now facing new challenges – corruption, economic disparity, and the question of how to achieve lasting peace and reconciliation.

Legacy of 1872

The 1872 election saw Grant defeat Greeley in a landslide victory. However, the divisions within the Republican Party and the nation remained. The issues of race, Reconstruction, and corruption continued to shape the political landscape for years to come.

The 1872 RNC, though lacking in suspense, serves as a stark reminder that even in moments of apparent political certainty, deeper currents of change and uncertainty are often simmering beneath the surface. It reminds us that the path of progress is rarely smooth, and that even the most unified fronts can fracture under the weight of internal divisions and external pressures.

1876: A Convention Forged in the Crucible of Reconstruction

The year 1876 marked a pivotal moment in American history. The wounds of the Civil War were still fresh, and the nation grappled with the immense challenges of Reconstruction. Amidst this turbulent backdrop, the Republican Party convened in Cincinnati, Ohio, to choose their standard-bearer for the upcoming presidential election.

Cincinnati: The Queen City Welcomes a Divided Nation

Cincinnati, dubbed the "Queen City of the West," was a bustling hub of commerce and industry in 1876. Its strategic location on the Ohio River made it a gateway between the North and South, reflecting the very divisions that the nation sought to heal. The city boasted a large German-American population, a demographic that largely sided with the Republican Party for its stance against slavery and its support for economic modernization.

The Republican National Convention was held at the Exposition Hall, a grand structure that could accommodate thousands of delegates and spectators. The city buzzed with excitement and anticipation as politicians, delegates, and journalists descended upon Cincinnati, each holding their breath for the drama that was sure to unfold.

Reconstruction and its Discontents: The Defining Issue

The predominant issue looming over the 1876 Republican National Convention was undoubtedly Reconstruction. The ambitious project of integrating the former Confederate states back into the Union and securing equal rights for freedmen faced fierce opposition from the South. The Democratic Party, resurgent after its wartime losses, exploited racial anxieties and resentment towards federal intervention in the South.

The Republican Party, itself, was divided on the best course of action. Moderates favored a gradual approach to Reconstruction, emphasizing economic development and reconciliation. Radicals, on the other hand, pushed for more aggressive federal intervention to protect black civil rights and punish former Confederates. This internal debate over Reconstruction played a crucial role in shaping the party platform and the eventual choice of the presidential nominee.

Titans of Politics: The Leaders Shaping the Nation

The Republican Party boasted a constellation of prominent figures in 1876. President Ulysses S. Grant, the Civil War hero who had overseen the early years of Reconstruction, was nearing the end of his second term. While immensely popular among Republicans, Grant's presidency had been marred by scandals and accusations of corruption, making his potential third-term bid a contentious issue.

Among the potential successors to Grant, several figures stood out. James G. Blaine, a charismatic Congressman from Maine, was a leading voice of the Republican Party and a champion of Radical Reconstruction. Roscoe Conkling, a powerful Senator from New York, commanded a loyal following within the party and was known for his sharp intellect and political maneuvering. Other prominent contenders included Rutherford B. Hayes, the Governor of Ohio, and Benjamin Bristow, Grant's Secretary of the Treasury. Each candidate represented different factions within the Republican Party, their ambitions and rivalries adding to the drama of the convention.

The Compromise Candidate: Hayes Emerges from the Fray

The 1876 Republican National Convention was a tightly contested affair. After several rounds of balloting, no clear frontrunner emerged. James G. Blaine, despite being the initial favorite, faced accusations of financial impropriety which hampered his chances. The convention became deadlocked, with no candidate securing the necessary majority.

It was in this atmosphere of political maneuvering and compromise that Rutherford B. Hayes emerged as the unexpected nominee. Hayes, a relatively unknown figure on the national stage, was seen as a compromise candidate who could potentially unite the different factions within the Republican Party. His reputation for honesty and his moderate stance on Reconstruction made him palatable to a broad spectrum of delegates.

Legacy of 1876: A Pyrrhic Victory and the End of Reconstruction

The 1876 presidential election proved to be one of the most controversial in American history. Hayes narrowly defeated his Democratic opponent, Samuel J. Tilden, in a contest marred by accusations of voter fraud and suppression. The outcome of the election was ultimately decided by a special electoral commission, which awarded the disputed electoral votes to Hayes.

The Compromise of 1877, which resolved the electoral crisis, effectively marked the end of Reconstruction. In exchange for Democratic acceptance of Hayes's presidency, federal troops were withdrawn from the South, leaving African Americans vulnerable to disenfranchisement and Jim Crow segregation.

The 1876 Republican National Convention, held in the heart of a nation still grappling with its past, ultimately set the stage for a tragic compromise that would have long-lasting consequences for American society. The hopes of a truly unified nation, where all citizens were granted equal rights and opportunities, were dashed against the rocks of political expediency. The legacy of 1876 served as a stark reminder of the fragility of democracy and the unfinished work of achieving true equality for all.

1880 - A Convention of Stalwarts, Half-Breeds, and a Dark Horse in Chicago

The year is 1880. The wounds of the Civil War, though slowly healing, still left deep scars across the nation. Reconstruction in the South was faltering, corruption cast a shadow over American politics, and the economy grappled with growing pains and currency debates. In the midst of this tumultuous backdrop, the Republican Party, still bearing the mantle of Lincoln, gathered in Chicago to choose their standard-bearer for the upcoming presidential election.

I. The Windy City Takes Center Stage

Chicago, a city rising from the ashes of the Great Fire just nine years prior, pulsated with a raw, determined energy. This burgeoning metropolis, already a hub of industry and trade, was eager to showcase its resilience and ambition on the national stage. The newly constructed Interstate Exposition Building, a testament to Chicago's indomitable spirit, was chosen as the venue for the Republican National Convention.

II. The Issues of the Day: A Nation in Flux

The nation in 1880 was a land of stark contrasts and simmering tensions. The fight for civil rights for African Americans continued in the face of rising Jim Crow laws in the South. The economy, while experiencing industrial growth, was plagued by financial instability, particularly around the debate between hard-money advocates, who favored a gold standard, and those who supported the continued circulation of paper money, known as "greenbacks." This debate had significant implications for farmers, laborers, and businesses alike.

III. Stalwarts, Half-Breeds, and a Divided Party

The Republican Party itself was deeply divided in 1880. Two main factions, the Stalwarts and the Half-Breeds, battled for control. The Stalwarts, led by the powerful Senator Roscoe Conkling of New York, represented the party's old guard. They favored traditional machine politics, patronage, and resisted civil service reform. The Half-Breeds, led by Senator James G. Blaine of Maine, presented themselves as reformers, advocating for merit-based civil service and a more moderate approach to Southern Reconstruction.

This internal division played out dramatically in the race for the Republican nomination. The front-runner was former President Ulysses S. Grant, a national hero but also a symbol of the Stalwart faction. Grant, seeking an unprecedented third term, had strong support from Conkling and his allies. However, Grant's two terms had been marred by scandals and accusations of corruption, making him a controversial figure for many within the party.

The Half-Breeds rallied behind James G. Blaine as their champion. Blaine, a charismatic orator and skilled politician, promised a break from the scandals of the Grant administration. However, he carried his own baggage, as he was dogged by accusations of financial impropriety from his time as Speaker of the House.

IV. A Dark Horse Emerges: The Rise of James A. Garfield

As the convention commenced, the tension between the Stalwarts and Half-Breeds reached a fever pitch. The first thirty-five ballots resulted in a deadlock. Grant held a strong lead, but he couldn't secure the majority needed to clinch the nomination. Blaine was a close second, but he too faced strong opposition from within the party.

It became evident that neither Grant nor Blaine could unite the party. A compromise candidate was needed, someone who could bridge the divide and offer a fresh start. Enter James A. Garfield, a Congressman from Ohio and a dark horse candidate who had garnered little attention in the early stages of the race.

Garfield, a Civil War hero and respected legislator, appealed to both factions. He had ties to the Half-Breeds through his support for civil service reform but was also seen as acceptable to the Stalwarts. On the 36th ballot, a wave of delegates shifted their support to Garfield, and he unexpectedly secured the Republican nomination for president.

V. The Aftermath: A Nation Chooses and an Assassination Rocks the Republic

The 1880 Republican National Convention stands as a testament to the unpredictable nature of American politics. The bitter rivalry between Stalwarts and Half-Breeds, the rise and fall of political giants, and the emergence of a dark horse candidate all make this convention a captivating chapter in American history. Garfield's nomination, born out of party division, proved to be a pivotal moment.

While the Republicans emerged from Chicago seemingly unified, the scars of the convention lingered. The issues that divided the party – civil service reform, the role of government in the economy, and the future of Reconstruction – continued to shape the political landscape for decades to come.

Garfield went on to win a close election against Democrat Winfield Scott Hancock. Tragically, his presidency was cut short. Just a few months into his term, Garfield was assassinated by a disgruntled office seeker, a stark reminder of the political violence that plagued the era. His assassination further fueled the debate over civil service reform, a cause Garfield himself championed.

The 1880 Republican National Convention, though often overshadowed by the tragedy that followed, offers a compelling glimpse into a nation struggling to define itself. It highlights the enduring power of political factions, the unpredictable nature of political conventions, and the profound impact that a single event can have on the course of American history.

1884: A Convention of Stalwarts and Half-Breeds

The year is 1884. America finds herself caught in the throes of immense change. The wounds of the Civil War, though slowly healing, still leave their mark. Industrialization roars across the land, birthing both prosperity and unsettling inequality. And in the bustling city of Chicago, a political drama unfolds, one that would shape the course of American politics for years to come. This is the story of the 1884 Republican National Convention, a gathering that pitted brother against brother, ideal against ambition, in a battle for the soul of the Grand Old Party.

Chicago: The City of Big Shoulders and Bigger Ambitions

Chicago, the pulsing heart of the Midwest, was a city on the rise. Having rebuilt with astonishing speed after the devastating fire of 1871, it now boasted a skyline studded with ambitious skyscrapers, a testament to the raw energy and boundless optimism of the age. The Republican Party, recognizing the city's growing influence and central location, chose Chicago as the stage for their grand convention. From June 3rd to 6th, 1884, the newly constructed Exposition Hall, an architectural marvel in itself, played host to over 800 delegates and countless spectators, all eager to witness history in the making.

A Nation Grappling with its Identity

The issues dominating the national discourse were as weighty as they were complex. Reconstruction, the ambitious project of stitching the nation back together after the Civil War, was faltering. Jim Crow laws were casting a long shadow over the South, while political corruption festered in both the North and South. The burgeoning labor movement was gaining momentum, demanding fair wages and better working conditions, often met with resistance from powerful industrialists. The Republican Party, once the champion of abolition and unity, found itself wrestling with these complex issues, its own identity caught in the crosshairs of progress and tradition.

The Titans of the Party: Blaine, Arthur, and the Shadow of Grant

The Republican Party of 1884 was a party divided. Two main factions, the Stalwarts and the Half-Breeds, battled for control, their rivalry embodying the ideological tensions gripping the nation. The Stalwarts, led by the powerful Senator Roscoe Conkling, clung to the old ways, advocating for patronage, political machines, and a less aggressive approach to civil service reform. The Half-Breeds, a more reform-minded faction, favored a merit-based system and a stronger stance against corruption.

At the heart of this power struggle stood two prominent figures: James G. Blaine, a charismatic senator from Maine, and Chester A. Arthur, the incumbent president. Blaine, a consummate politician and darling of the Half-Breeds, had narrowly lost the 1880 nomination to James A. Garfield, only to ascend to the presidency after Garfield's assassination. He sought the nomination once more, his ambition fueled by a burning desire to finally grasp the nation's highest office.

Arthur, a former Stalwart thrust into the presidency by tragedy, surprised many by governing as a reformer, distancing himself from the very faction that had propelled him to power. He remained a long-shot contender for the nomination, his candidacy hampered by ill health and the lingering suspicion of his Stalwart past.

Adding further intrigue to the proceedings was the specter of Ulysses S. Grant, the nation's iconic Civil War hero and two-term president. While Grant himself harbored no desire for a third term, a powerful contingent of Stalwarts, hoping to capitalize on his enduring popularity, sought to draft him as the nominee.

A Contentious Convention and a Fateful Nomination

The 1884 Republican National Convention was a spectacle unlike any other. The fight for the nomination was fierce and dramatic. Blaine, commanding the loyalty of a large portion of the delegates, fought tooth and nail against accusations of corruption stemming from his past dealings with railroad companies. Arthur, though lacking Blaine's charisma and political machinery, remained a formidable contender, his candidacy buoyed by a record of integrity and reform.

The first ballot set the tone for the tense days to come. Blaine emerged as the frontrunner with a significant lead, yet he fell short of the required majority. Arthur trailed behind, while John Sherman, a respected senator from Ohio, and other minor candidates garnered the remaining votes. As the balloting continued, the drama intensified. The "Plumed Knight," as Blaine was known, saw his support steadily increase, while Arthur's hopes dwindled. The Grant movement, failing to gain traction, fizzled out after a few rounds.

Finally, on the fourth ballot, James G. Blaine secured the Republican nomination. The convention hall erupted in a cacophony of cheers and boos, reflecting the deep divisions within the party. While Blaine emerged victorious, the scars of the battle remained. Many Stalwarts, disillusioned by Blaine's victory, refused to support him in the general election, ultimately contributing to his narrow defeat at the hands of Grover Cleveland, the Democratic nominee.

The Legacy of 1884: A Turning Point for the GOP

The 1884 Republican National Convention, a microcosm of the political and social currents of the era, proved to be a turning point for the Grand Old Party. The bitter battle between the Stalwarts and Half-Breeds, the rise of reform as a central issue, and the prominence of personalities like Blaine and Arthur, all foreshadowed the evolving landscape of American politics. The convention, while ultimately delivering a victory for Blaine and the Half-Breeds, revealed deep fissures within the party that would continue to shape its identity in the years to come. The Republican Party, born out of the fight against slavery, now found itself grappling with the complexities of a rapidly industrializing nation, seeking to balance its commitment to individual liberty with the demands of a changing economic order. The echoes of the 1884 convention, with its mix of high drama, political intrigue, and ideological battles, would continue to resonate long after the last delegate had left Chicago, shaping the destiny of the Republican Party and, indeed, the nation itself.

1888: A Convention of Titans in Chicago

Chicago, the "Windy City," pulsated with a different kind of energy in June 1888. Recovering from the devastating Haymarket affair of 1886 and brimming with the ambition of a burgeoning metropolis, the city played host to a Republican National Convention brimming with political heavyweights and contentious issues. The stakes were high, the atmosphere electric, and the decisions made within the walls of the Chicago Auditorium would reverberate through the halls of American history.

A Nation in Transition

The 1888 election unfolded against the backdrop of a nation grappling with rapid industrialization, labor unrest, and a burgeoning urban-rural divide. The echoes of the Civil War were fading, replaced by new anxieties about economic inequality, immigration, and the role of government in regulating the burgeoning industrial behemoths.

The incumbent Democratic President Grover Cleveland had surprised many by advocating for civil service reform and challenging powerful corporate interests. However, his stance on tariffs ignited fierce opposition, particularly from industrialists who benefited from protectionist policies. This single issue, the tariff, became a defining fault line in American politics and took center stage at the 1888 Republican National Convention.

The Leaders and their Legacies

The Republican Party, eager to reclaim the White House after four years, boasted a roster of prominent figures. James G. Blaine, the party's charismatic but controversial 1884 nominee, loomed large despite his declared intention not to seek the nomination again. His ardent supporters, dubbed the "Plumed Knights," remained a powerful force within the party.

Senator John Sherman of Ohio, a financial expert and architect of the Sherman Antitrust Act, was considered a frontrunner. His long record of public service and moderate stance appealed to many, but he lacked the popular appeal of some of his rivals.

Then there was the dark horse candidate, former Senator Benjamin Harrison of Indiana. A Civil War general and grandson of President William Henry Harrison, he represented a blend of military pedigree and Midwestern pragmatism. While not a captivating orator, his strong stance on the tariff resonated with industrialists and working-class voters concerned about job security.

The Drama Unfolds: Contested Nominations and Backroom Deals

The 1888 Convention was a battleground of political maneuvering. Blaine's shadow hung over the proceedings, with many delegates hoping he would reconsider his decision and accept a draft. His refusal to do so left the convention in a deadlock.

Sherman led on the first ballot but lacked the necessary majority. The subsequent rounds saw a flurry of backroom negotiations, with state delegations switching allegiances and whispers of political deals filling the air. Harrison, strategically positioned by his campaign manager, the shrewd political operative Matthew Quay, gradually gained momentum.

A Defining Moment: Harrison's Nomination and the Tariff Takes Center Stage

After eight grueling ballots, Benjamin Harrison finally secured the Republican nomination. The convention, however, had cemented the issue that would dominate the general election: the tariff.

The Republican platform, crafted with input from powerful industrialists like Andrew Carnegie, explicitly advocated for high protective tariffs. This stance contrasted sharply with the Democrats' call for tariff reduction, setting the stage for a fiercely contested election centered on the nation's economic future.

The 1888 RNC and its Impact on American History

The 1888 Republican National Convention was more than just a political gathering; it was a microcosm of a nation in flux. The issues debated, the alliances forged, and the decisions made reverberated far beyond the convention hall.

Harrison's subsequent victory in the general election ushered in a period of Republican dominance. The McKinley Tariff Act of 1890, a direct result of the party's stance solidified at the convention, further escalated the tariff debate, deepening the political divide and shaping the economic landscape for years to come.

The 1888 Convention also underscored the growing influence of powerful industrialists in American politics. Their financial backing and lobbying efforts played a significant role in shaping the Republican platform, demonstrating the increasing entanglement of business interests and political power, a dynamic that would continue to shape American society throughout the Gilded Age and beyond.

1892 - A City of Steel and the Seeds of Discontent

Minneapolis: Flour Power and a Glimpse of the Future

The year was 1892, and the Republican Party, riding high on a wave of economic prosperity for some, chose the bustling city of Minneapolis, Minnesota, as the stage for its national convention. Minneapolis, often nicknamed the "Mill City," was a symbol of American industry and innovation, renowned for its flour mills that processed the bounty of the Great Plains. The city, straddling the banks of the Mississippi River, presented a stark contrast to the genteel, more established cities that typically hosted such grand political events.

The choice of Minneapolis was no accident. The Republican Party sought to project an image of dynamism and progress, aligning itself with the burgeoning industries of the Midwest. The city, with its wide avenues and ambitious skyline punctuated by grain elevators and flour mills, provided the perfect backdrop. The convention itself took place in the

Industrial Exposition Building, a colossal structure showcasing the latest in American ingenuity – a fitting stage for a party that prided itself on its role in the nation's economic growth.

A Nation in Transition

Beneath the veneer of progress and prosperity, however, simmered a cauldron of anxieties and discontent. The United States in 1892 was a nation in the throes of rapid transformation. The Industrial Revolution, while fueling economic growth, also spawned labor unrest, income inequality, and a widening gap between the rich and poor. Farmers, burdened by falling crop prices and rising railroad rates, increasingly viewed the Republican Party, often seen as beholden to industrial interests, with suspicion.

The political landscape mirrored this societal ferment. The Populist movement, advocating for the interests of farmers and laborers, was gaining traction, posing a significant challenge to the established order. The Democrats, sensing an opportunity, nominated the charismatic Grover Cleveland, who had served as president from 1885 to 1889, for a non-consecutive second term. Cleveland, known for his fiscal conservatism and opposition to high tariffs, presented a formidable challenge to the Republican nominee.

The Incumbent and the Rising Star

The incumbent president and Republican nominee, Benjamin Harrison, was a stark contrast to his predecessor. Reserved and scholarly, Harrison lacked

53

Cleveland's common touch but possessed a keen intellect and a deep understanding of policy. While Harrison could point to a successful record on issues like civil rights and the modernization of the navy, he struggled to connect with ordinary Americans.

Within the Republican Party itself, a new generation of leaders was emerging. Men like Theodore Roosevelt, then serving on the Civil Service Commission, and William McKinley, a congressman from Ohio, represented a more progressive wing of the party, advocating for social reforms and greater government regulation of industry. Their presence signaled a growing rift between the old guard and those who believed the party needed to adapt to the changing realities of American life.

A Convention Divided

The 1892 Republican National Convention reflected this sense of unease and uncertainty. The issue of the protective tariff, a cornerstone of Republican economic policy, proved particularly divisive. While industrialists and factory workers in the Northeast benefited from tariffs that shielded them from foreign competition, farmers in the Midwest viewed them as harmful to their interests. The debate over the tariff exposed the growing sectional divisions within the party and the nation.

The convention also saw a spirited, albeit unsuccessful, challenge to Harrison's renomination. James G. Blaine, Harrison's Secretary of State and a popular figure within the party, emerged as the candidate of those dissatisfied with Harrison's leadership. Blaine, however, withdrew his name from contention, and Harrison secured the nomination on the first ballot. The lack of genuine excitement surrounding Harrison's nomination, however, hinted at the challenges that lay ahead.

Legacy of Doubt

The 1892 Republican National Convention, held amidst the industrial grandeur of Minneapolis, marked a turning point in American political history. The seeds of discontent sown during this period of rapid economic and social change would eventually blossom into the Progressive Era reforms of the early 20th century. The convention itself, though ultimately resulting in the renomination of a sitting president, exposed the growing divisions within the Republican Party and American society as a whole – divisions that would continue to shape the nation's political landscape for decades to come.

Though the Republicans presented a united front, the unconvincing victory in Minneapolis foreshadowed the general election. Harrison's loss to Cleveland just a few months later demonstrated the growing strength of the populist movement and the public's desire for change. The 1892 convention serves as a reminder that even in moments of apparent triumph, underlying currents of discontent can have a profound and lasting impact on the course of a nation.

The Crossroads of 1896 - St. Louis and the Rise of Big Business

The 1896 Republican National Convention, held in the bustling city of St. Louis, Missouri, stands as a pivotal moment in American political history. It was a convention that reflected the anxieties and divisions of a nation grappling with economic depression, social unrest, and the burgeoning influence of industrial capitalism. In the shadow of the Gateway Arch yet to be built, the Republican party would choose a path that would shape the nation's trajectory for decades to come.

A Nation in Flux

The years leading up to 1896 were tumultuous. The Panic of 1893 had plunged the United States into a severe economic depression. Unemployment skyrocketed, farmers grappled with falling crop prices and crushing debt, and labor strikes, like the Pullman Strike of 1894, highlighted the growing tensions between workers and industrialists.

This backdrop of economic hardship fueled a national debate about the role of government in addressing the plight of the working class and regulating the growing power of corporations. The Populist movement, with its calls for free silver coinage, government ownership of railroads, and other reforms, gained significant traction, particularly in the West and South. Their rise posed a direct challenge to the two established parties, the Democrats and the Republicans.

The Republican Landscape

Within the Republican Party, a deep fissure existed on the issue of monetary policy. The pro-silver faction, largely composed of farmers and silver miners, favored bimetallism – a system where both gold and silver backed the U.S. dollar. They argued this would increase the money supply, inflate prices, and offer them relief from their debts.

Conversely, the pro-gold faction, primarily industrialists and financiers from the Northeast, championed the gold standard as the path to economic stability and international credibility. They saw free silver as inflationary and reckless, a threat to their financial interests.

Leading figures within the Republican Party reflected this divide. The "Plumed Knight," Senator James G. Blaine of Maine, though not a candidate in 1896 due to failing health, cast a long shadow over the proceedings. A champion of protectionist tariffs and a strong navy, Blaine's charismatic leadership and moderate stance on silver made him a kingmaker within the party.

57

On the opposing side stood the rising star of Ohio, Governor William McKinley. A staunch supporter of the gold standard, McKinley represented the interests of big business and industrial growth. His campaign manager, Mark Hanna, a wealthy industrialist himself, orchestrated a sophisticated and well-funded campaign that capitalized on McKinley's message of economic prosperity tied to the gold standard.

The St. Louis Convention

The St. Louis Exposition and Music Hall, draped in patriotic bunting and illuminated by electric lights (a novelty at the time), played host to the Republican National Convention. Thousands of delegates, alternates, journalists, and spectators descended upon the city, eager to witness the political drama unfold.

The convention saw impassioned speeches on tariffs, foreign policy, and veterans' pensions, but the defining issue remained the currency question. The platform debate became a battle for the soul of the Republican Party. The pro-silver faction, led by fiery orator William Jennings Bryan, fought tooth and nail for their cause. However, McKinley's forces, backed by Hanna's well-oiled political machine, emerged victorious.

The Republican platform adopted in St. Louis declared unequivocal support for the gold standard. The party broke definitively with its agrarian roots and embraced the burgeoning industrial future. This pivotal decision alienated many farmers and working-class Republicans who felt abandoned by the party they once championed.

The Aftermath and Legacy

The nomination of William McKinley, a staunch advocate of the gold standard and protective tariffs, solidified the Republican party's transformation into the party of big business. His subsequent victory in the general election against the Democratic and Populist nominee, William Jennings Bryan, marked the beginning of a Republican era that would last, with a brief interruption, for the next three decades.

The 1896 election, shaped by the decisions made in that St. Louis convention hall, proved to be a realigning election in American history. The Republicans' embrace of industrial capitalism and the gold standard ushered in an era of unprecedented economic growth and corporate power, but it also exacerbated the growing divide between the rich and the poor, setting the stage for the progressive reforms of the 20th century. The ghosts of St. Louis, the echoes of those heated debates over silver and gold, continued to reverberate in American politics for decades to come.

1900 - A Convention of Prosperity and Empire

Philadelphia and the Dawn of the American Century

The year 1900 dawned with a sense of optimism and boundless potential in America. The nation, having just emerged victorious from the Spanish-American War, found itself on the cusp of a new century and a new global role. It was in this climate of expansionism and burgeoning industrial might that the Republican National Convention convened in Philadelphia, Pennsylvania, from June 19th to 21st.

Philadelphia, the birthplace of the nation, provided a symbolic backdrop for the Republicans to showcase their vision for the future. The city, bustling with commerce and industry, served as a potent reminder of the party's commitment to economic growth and prosperity. The convention itself was held in the imposing Exposition Auditorium, a testament to the architectural ambition of the age.

Echoes of War and the Rise of Progressivism

While the Spanish-American War had concluded in 1898, its aftershocks reverberated through the political landscape. The conflict had thrust the United States onto the world stage, leaving it in control of new territories like the Philippines, Puerto Rico, and Guam. The question of how to manage these new acquisitions and define America's role as a global power became a central debate, both within the Republican party and the nation at large.

Domestically, the dawn of the 20th century witnessed the burgeoning Progressive movement gaining momentum. Issues like social justice, labor rights, and government regulation of big business began to take center stage. While the Republican party, traditionally aligned with business interests, grappled with these emerging concerns, the seeds of future internal divisions were sown.

Familiar Faces and Rising Stars

The 1900 Republican National Convention saw the culmination of William McKinley's first term as President. Having successfully navigated the country through an economic depression and a foreign war, McKinley enjoyed immense popularity. His renomination was a foregone conclusion. As such, the real drama of the convention lay in the selection of the Vice President.

The incumbent Vice President, Garret Hobart, had died in office in 1899, leaving a void on the ticket. Several prominent figures were considered for the position, including Senator William Allison of Iowa and Senator Theodore Roosevelt of New York. Roosevelt, a charismatic war hero and former Assistant Secretary of the Navy, had gained national recognition for his leadership of the Rough Riders during the Spanish-American War.

A Calculated Gamble and a Twist of Fate

While Roosevelt's popularity made him an attractive candidate, his progressive leanings made him a risky choice for the conservative wing of the party. Many party bosses, wary of his reformist zeal, preferred the more predictable Allison. However, powerful forces, including New York Senator Thomas Platt, saw an opportunity to sideline Roosevelt's political ambitions by pushing him towards the perceived dead-end of the Vice Presidency.

The convention ultimately nominated Roosevelt as McKinley's running mate. The decision was a gamble for both sides. Roosevelt, while initially reluctant, saw an opportunity to advance his political career, while the party bosses underestimated his ambition and the unpredictable hand of fate.

A Legacy Forged in Tragedy

The 1900 Republican National Convention, though seemingly a straightforward affair, had profound consequences for the future of the United States. The nomination of Theodore Roosevelt as Vice President, orchestrated as a political maneuver, would have unexpected and far-reaching implications.

Six months into McKinley's second term, an assassin's bullet would cut his life short. Theodore Roosevelt, the young and energetic Vice President, would ascend to the presidency, ushering in an era of progressive reform and cementing the United States' place as a global power. The events of 1900, decided amidst the grandeur of the Philadelphia convention, would shape the destiny of a nation on the brink of its own "American Century."

1904: A Coronation in Chicago

The year 1904 saw the Republican National Convention descend upon Chicago, a city still bearing the scars of the Great Fire of 1871, yet pulsing with the energy of a nation entering a new century. The choice of Chicago, a hub of industry and commerce, reflected the Republican Party's image as the party of prosperity and progress. The convention itself, held from June 21st to 23rd, would prove to be more of a coronation than a contest, solidifying Theodore Roosevelt's hold on the nation's highest office.

The Spirit of the Age: Progress and its Discontents

The dawn of the 20th century was a time of immense change and contradictions. America, having flexed its muscles on the world stage with the Spanish-American War, was grappling with its newfound status as an imperial power. The Progressive movement, gaining momentum across the country, sought to address the ills of industrialization and urbanization – poverty, corruption, and social injustice.

The Republican Party, under Roosevelt's leadership, found itself navigating these turbulent waters. While embracing economic expansion and industrial growth, Roosevelt, a progressive himself, recognized the need for regulation and reform. His "Square Deal" promised fairness for all Americans, seeking to curb the excesses of big business while ensuring continued economic prosperity.

The Protagonists: Roosevelt and the Republican Guard

Theodore Roosevelt, having ascended to the Presidency after the assassination of William McKinley, was already a force to be reckoned with. Charismatic, energetic, and deeply popular, he embodied the spirit of the age. His commitment to conservation, trust-busting, and labor rights resonated with a public hungry for reform.

The Republican Party of 1904 was a diverse mix of old guard stalwarts and progressive reformers. Stalwarts like Mark Hanna, the powerful Ohio Senator, still wielded considerable influence, representing the interests of traditional business interests. On the other hand, progressives like Robert La Follette, the firebrand Governor of Wisconsin, pushed for greater government intervention in the economy and social welfare programs.

A Foregone Conclusion: The Nomination

The 1904 Republican National Convention was a carefully orchestrated affair. Roosevelt, already in the White House, faced no serious opposition. His nomination was a foregone conclusion, and the convention served primarily as a platform to showcase his popularity and solidify his control over the party.

1908: A Changing Nation Chooses Stability - Chicago's Grand Spectacle

The year 1908 dawned with a sense of both anticipation and uncertainty in the United States. The nation, deeply entrenched in the Progressive Era, grappled with issues of industrialization, urbanization, and social reform. The outgoing Republican President, Theodore Roosevelt, a figure both revered and reviled for his trust-busting and conservation efforts, had chosen not to seek a third term, leaving a power vacuum at the top. Against this backdrop, the Republican National Convention of 1908, held in the bustling metropolis of Chicago, promised to be a pivotal event, shaping the future direction of the country.

The "Windy City" Takes Center Stage

Chicago, with its booming stockyards and burgeoning population, served as a microcosm of the rapid changes sweeping across the nation. The city, still rebuilding from the devastating Great Fire of 1871, had emerged as a symbol of American resilience and industrial might. The newly constructed Chicago Coliseum, a behemoth structure boasting the largest indoor arena in the world, was chosen to host the convention, its grandeur reflecting the ambitions of a party seeking to retain its grip on power.

The Issues: Prosperity, Progress, and Protection

The 1908 Republican National Convention unfolded amidst a complex interplay of national issues. The economy, recovering from the Panic of 1907, remained a top concern for many Americans. Labor unrest, fueled by unsafe working conditions and growing income inequality, simmered beneath the surface of the burgeoning industrial machine. The progressive movement, advocating for social justice and government regulation of big business, gained momentum, challenging the laissez-faire approach favored by many within the Republican establishment.

Titans of the Party and the Weight of Legacy

The shadow of Theodore Roosevelt loomed large over the convention. While absent from the ballot, his presence was palpable as delegates debated the merits of continuing his progressive policies. William Howard Taft, Roosevelt's handpicked successor and the sitting Secretary of War, emerged as the frontrunner. A seasoned jurist and administrator, Taft represented a continuation of the Republican establishment, advocating for cautious reform and economic stability.

He faced opposition from various factions within the party. Conservative Republicans, wary of Roosevelt's progressive zeal, rallied behind Speaker of the House Joseph Gurney Cannon, a staunch advocate for limited government and business interests. Senator Robert La Follette of Wisconsin, a fiery progressive reformer, campaigned on a platform of greater government intervention, challenging both Taft's moderation and Cannon's conservatism.

The Drama Unfolds: Backroom Deals and Rousing Speeches

The 1908 Republican National Convention was not without its share of political intrigue. Behind closed doors, deals were struck and alliances forged as candidates jockeyed for position. The battle for the Republican nomination largely came down to Taft and La Follette. La Follette, with his impassioned speeches championing the common man, energized the progressive wing of the party. However, Taft, bolstered by Roosevelt's endorsement and the support of the party establishment, ultimately prevailed.

The convention witnessed moments of high drama, particularly during the platform debates. The issue of tariff reform, a cornerstone of the progressive agenda, sparked heated exchanges on the convention floor. La Follette's impassioned plea for tariff reductions, aimed at curbing the power of trusts, was met with fierce resistance from conservative Republicans, highlighting the deep divisions within the party.

The Choice: A Promise of Continuity

On June 20th, 1908, after four days of intense debate and political maneuvering, William Howard Taft secured the Republican nomination for President of the United States. The convention concluded with a rousing display of party unity, showcasing Taft as the heir apparent to Roosevelt's legacy. The platform adopted by the party reflected a delicate balance between the progressive and conservative wings, promising both continuity and cautious reform.

The 1908 RNC and its Place in History

The Republican National Convention of 1908 stands as a significant marker in American political history. It marked the end of an era, closing the chapter on Theodore Roosevelt's impactful presidency. Yet, it also served as a bridge to the future, ushering in a period of continued reform under Taft. While overshadowed by other tumultuous conventions in American history, the 1908 gathering offered a glimpse into a nation grappling with profound change, striving to reconcile its burgeoning industrial might with the demands of social justice and economic equality. The echoes of those debates continue to resonate even today, a testament to the enduring legacy of the 1908 Republican National Convention.

1912: A House Divided - Chicago's Contentious Convention

The year 1912 was a tumultuous one in American politics. The nation, on the brink of social and economic change, watched with bated breath as the Republican Party gathered in Chicago for its National Convention. Little did anyone know, this gathering would become a pivotal chapter in the story of the Republican Party and, indeed, the United States.

Chicago: The City of Big Shoulders and Bigger Ambitions

Chicago, the bustling metropolis of the Midwest, was no stranger to hosting grand political spectacles. Having previously hosted the Republican National Convention in 1860, 1880, and 1884, the city was known for its robust political atmosphere and impressive infrastructure. The 1912 convention took place in the colossal Chicago Coliseum, a behemoth of a building capable of accommodating tens of thousands of spectators. This choice reflected the scale of the political drama about to unfold.

A Nation on the Cusp of Change: The Issues at Stake

The Progressive Era was in full swing, and the nation grappled with issues of social justice, economic inequality, and corporate power. Labor rights, women's suffrage, and government regulation of monopolies were hotly debated topics, dividing the nation and the Republican Party itself.

Two Wings, One Party: The Republican Party was deeply divided between its conservative and progressive wings. The incumbent President, William Howard Taft, represented the conservative establishment. He advocated for limited government intervention in business and a cautious approach to social reforms. In stark contrast, the charismatic former President, Theodore Roosevelt, had returned from his African safari energized and ready to champion progressive ideals.

The Contenders: A Battle of Ideologies

The Incumbent: William Howard Taft, despite inheriting Roosevelt's mantle in 1908, had alienated many progressives within the party through his perceived conservatism. He entered the convention with the support of the party machinery, but his hold on the nomination was far from secure.

The Challenger: Theodore Roosevelt, a force of nature and political titan, had thrown his hat back into the ring, challenging Taft for the Republican nomination. Roosevelt championed his "New Nationalism" platform, promising sweeping reforms to address social injustices and curb the power of large corporations.

The Compromise (that wasn't): Robert La Follette, the progressive Senator from Wisconsin, emerged as a third option for those who saw both Taft and Roosevelt as flawed candidates. La Follette, a champion of labor rights and direct democracy, hoped to unite the progressive wing under his banner.

The Convention Explodes: A Week of Tumult

From June 18th to 22nd, 1912, the Chicago Coliseum became a battleground. The battle lines were drawn not only between Taft and Roosevelt but also between the old guard of party bosses and the rising tide of grassroots activism.

Roosevelt's Triumph, Taft's Victory: The convention saw intense procedural battles over contested delegates, accusations of fraud, and passionate speeches that captivated the nation. While Roosevelt won the majority of the delegate votes, the party leadership, firmly in Taft's control, maneuvered to secure his renomination.

A Party Divided Cannot Stand: Feeling cheated by the process, Roosevelt and his supporters bolted from the Republican Party, forming the Progressive Party, also known as the "Bull Moose Party." This split within the Republican ranks would have profound consequences.

The Aftermath: A Legacy of Reform and Division

The 1912 Republican National Convention, marred by infighting and acrimony, irrevocably changed the course of American political history. The schism within the Republican Party paved the way for the election of Democrat Woodrow Wilson, ending years of Republican dominance.

A Progressive Legacy: Despite Roosevelt's defeat, the progressive ideals championed at the convention continued to shape the nation's political landscape. Many of the reforms advocated by the progressives, such as women's suffrage, labor rights, and anti-trust legislation, were eventually enacted in the years following the 1912 election.

A Cautionary Tale: The 1912 convention serves as a stark reminder of the dangers of political division and the importance of party unity. The Republican Party's inability to bridge the gap between its conservative and progressive wings ultimately led to its downfall and ushered in a new era of Democratic leadership.

The echoes of the 1912 Republican National Convention resonate even today. It highlights the enduring tension between pragmatism and idealism, the challenges of managing internal party divisions, and the profound impact such divisions can have on the fate of a nation.

1916: A Convention Under the Shadow of War

Chicago's Second Act: A City Embraces the Elephant

The year was 1916. The "Great War," as it was known then, raged across Europe, casting a long shadow over the United States. As the nation grappled with its role on the world stage, the Republican Party descended upon Chicago for its eleventh National Convention, seeking a candidate to challenge the incumbent Democratic President, Woodrow Wilson.

This marked the second time Chicago hosted the Republican National Convention, the first being the tumultuous 1860 convention that nominated Abraham Lincoln. The city, by then a bustling metropolis and the heart of the Midwest, was eager to showcase its growth and influence. The convention took place at the Chicago Coliseum, a massive structure that could accommodate thousands of delegates and spectators. The city buzzed with political energy, anticipation hanging thick in the air.

A Nation Divided: The Issues of 1916

The political landscape of 1916 was dominated by a singular question: Should the United States remain neutral in the face of the devastating conflict in Europe? President Woodrow Wilson had campaigned on a platform of peace and neutrality, a message that resonated with many Americans weary of war.

However, the sinking of the Lusitania, a British ocean liner carrying American passengers, by a German U-boat in 1915, ignited public outrage and fueled calls for American intervention. The Republican Party found itself divided on the issue. Some, like former President Theodore Roosevelt, advocated for "preparedness" – a significant strengthening of the military in anticipation of potential US involvement. Others, however, clung to the traditional isolationist stance of the party, advocating for continued neutrality.

Beyond the war, other important issues simmered. Labor unrest was growing, fueled by poor working conditions and low wages. Women's suffrage was gaining momentum, with activists demanding the right to vote. The Progressive movement, though weakened after Roosevelt's defeat in 1912, continued to advocate for social and economic reforms.

The Players: Familiar Faces and Rising Stars

The Republican field was crowded with prominent figures. Former President Theodore Roosevelt, a towering figure within the party, loomed large despite initially declining to run. Many Republicans, dissatisfied with Wilson's perceived weakness on foreign policy and longing for a return to Roosevelt's progressive yet robust leadership, saw him as the only hope to defeat the incumbent president.

However, Roosevelt's animosity towards his handpicked successor, the incumbent Republican President William Howard Taft, who he felt had betrayed his progressive legacy, lingered. This animosity played a significant role in the Republican Party's schism in the 1912 election, leading to the formation of the Progressive Party, also known as the "Bull Moose Party," by Roosevelt's supporters.

Another prominent contender was Charles Evans Hughes, the Associate Justice of the Supreme Court. Hughes, a moderate with a reputation for integrity and intelligence, appealed to those seeking a less divisive figure than Roosevelt.

The convention also saw the rise of a young, ambitious senator from Indiana, Harry S. Truman, who served as a delegate. While Truman wouldn't achieve national prominence for several decades, his experience at the 1916 convention offered an early glimpse into the world of national politics.

The Nomination: A Compromise That Failed to Ignite

The 1916 Republican National Convention unfolded against a backdrop of tense negotiations and political maneuvering. Roosevelt, despite his initial reluctance, was eventually persuaded to seek the nomination.

However, his fiery rhetoric and aggressive foreign policy stance alienated many moderate Republicans.

Hughes, a more moderate figure, emerged as a compromise candidate. He secured the nomination on the tenth ballot, promising to uphold American rights and maintain peace. Charles Warren Fairbanks, a former senator from Indiana, became his running mate.

However, the convention failed to unite the Republican Party fully. Many Roosevelt supporters, disillusioned by the rejection of their leader, refused to support Hughes. The lack of unity within the party would have lasting consequences, hindering Hughes' chances in the general election.

Legacy of 1916: A Missed Opportunity and the Shifting Tides of History

The 1916 Republican National Convention, despite its excitement and political drama, is often overshadowed in history by the momentous events of the First World War. Hughes lost a close election to Woodrow Wilson, who successfully campaigned on a platform of peace and neutrality.

However, the convention marked a turning point in American political history. The Republican Party, deeply divided over the issue of American involvement in the war, struggled to find common ground. This division within the party reflected a larger national debate about America's role in the world, a debate that would continue to shape American foreign policy for decades to come.

Furthermore, the 1916 convention highlighted the shifting tides within the Republican Party. The Progressive era, with its emphasis on social and economic reforms, was coming to an end. A new generation of Republicans, more focused on business interests and less inclined towards government intervention, began to emerge. This shift would have profound implications for the Republican Party and the nation, paving the way for the conservative ascendancy of the 1920s.

1920: A Return to "Normalcy" in Chicago

The roar of the Roaring Twenties was still a low rumble as the Republican National Convention descended upon Chicago in June of 1920. The "Windy City," notorious for its vibrant energy and political maneuvering, provided a fitting backdrop for a nation grappling with the aftermath of a world war and searching for direction in a new decade. The 1920 Republican National Convention, held from June 8th to 12th, would become a pivotal moment in American history, shaping not only the political landscape but also the course of the nation's future.

A Nation in Transition

The United States in 1920 was a nation in flux, struggling to emerge from the shadow of World War I. The aftershocks of the conflict—economic instability, social unrest, and a fervent desire to retreat from global affairs—reverberated throughout society. The war had exposed deep divisions, and the country yearned for a return to stability. This longing for a simpler time resonated in the Republican Party's campaign slogan, "A

Return to Normalcy," a phrase coined by their eventual presidential nominee.

The Issues that Defined an Era

Several key issues dominated the national conversation and the platforms of both major parties:

- **The League of Nations:** Perhaps the most contentious issue was America's role in the newly formed League of Nations. President Woodrow Wilson, a Democrat, had championed the international organization, but it faced stiff opposition from Republicans, who viewed it as a threat to American sovereignty.

- **Prohibition:** The 18th Amendment, enacting Prohibition, had been ratified in January 1919. While both parties officially supported the amendment, enforcement and its social and economic consequences were hotly debated.

- **Women's Suffrage:** The 19th Amendment, granting women the right to vote, was on the verge of ratification, finally becoming law in August 1920. While a landmark achievement, its implementation and the role of women in the electorate were still being defined.

- **Economic Anxiety:** Post-war inflation, labor strikes, and fears of a recession fueled economic anxiety among Americans. Republicans campaigned on promises of prosperity and stability.

The 1920 Republican National Convention witnessed a cast of prominent figures vying for influence and the coveted presidential nomination:

- **Theodore Roosevelt:** Although not a candidate himself (he tragically passed away in 1919), the legacy of the former president and Republican icon loomed large. His progressive ideals still resonated with a segment of the party, while others favored a more conservative approach.

- **General Leonard Wood:** A hero of the Spanish-American War and a close confidante of Theodore Roosevelt, Wood was a frontrunner for the nomination. He represented the conservative wing of the party and appealed to those seeking a strong, experienced leader.

- **Governor Frank Lowden of Illinois:** Lowden, a successful businessman turned politician, was another formidable contender. He gained popularity for his efficient administration and fiscal conservatism.

- **Senator Hiram Johnson of California:** A progressive firebrand and fierce critic of the League of Nations, Johnson appealed to those seeking a return to isolationism and a focus on domestic issues.

- **Senator Warren G. Harding of Ohio:** Initially considered a long-shot, Harding was a relatively unknown senator with a talent for delivering eloquent speeches. His message of "normalcy" and his inoffensive, consensus-building style would ultimately prove appealing to a nation weary of division.

Deadlock and the Rise of Harding

The 1920 Republican National Convention was marked by a fierce battle for delegates and a protracted deadlock. None of the leading candidates were able to secure the necessary majority. As the balloting dragged on, backroom deals and political maneuvering intensified. Finally, on the tenth ballot, after days of intense negotiations, Warren G. Harding emerged as the compromise candidate, securing the Republican nomination for president.

A Convention of Firsts and Lasts

The 1920 Republican National Convention was not only significant for its political outcomes but also for several notable firsts and lasts:

- **First Convention Broadcast by Radio:** While still in its infancy, radio played a role in broadcasting portions of the convention proceedings, marking a significant step in the evolution of political communication.

- **Last Convention to Nominate a President from the Senate Directly:** Harding's nomination marked the final time a sitting senator would ascend directly to the presidency. Future presidential hopefuls from the Senate would generally serve as Vice President or governor before seeking the highest office.

The Legacy of the 1920 Convention

The 1920 Republican National Convention, while perhaps overshadowed in the annals of history by more dramatic gatherings, left an indelible mark on the United States. The choice of Warren G. Harding, with his message of "normalcy" and his conservative policies, ushered in a decade characterized by economic prosperity, social change, and a retreat from global engagement.

While Harding's presidency would later be tarnished by scandal, the 1920 convention laid the groundwork for a period of Republican dominance that would last for the majority of the 1920s. The desire for stability and a return to pre-war values, so palpable in the convention hall in Chicago, reflected the mood of the nation and shaped the political landscape for years to come.

1924: A Convention of Chaos and Compromise

The Roaring Twenties were in full swing as Republicans descended upon Cleveland, Ohio, for their 1924 National Convention. The city, a bustling hub of industry and progress, seemed a fitting backdrop for a party that prided itself on prosperity and progress. However, beneath the surface of economic boom and flapper dresses, deep divisions festered within the nation and the Republican party itself. The shadow of the recently deceased Woodrow Wilson loomed large, his progressive legacy a point of contention within Republican ranks. This chapter delves into the tumultuous events of the 1924 Republican National Convention, exploring the key players, issues, and lasting impact of this pivotal moment in American political history.

A Nation at a Crossroads

The United States in 1924 was grappling with the aftermath of World War I and the social and economic changes it had wrought. The war had propelled the US to a position of global power, yet a wave of isolationism was sweeping the nation. The economy was booming, but farmers struggled amidst falling crop prices. Urbanization was transforming American society, leading to cultural clashes between traditional and modern values. The issue of Prohibition, enacted in 1920, further divided Americans along moral and cultural lines.

The Republican Divide

These national tensions were mirrored within the Republican party. Two main factions vied for control: the conservative "Old Guard," led by aging titans like Senator Henry Cabot Lodge and former President William Howard Taft (now Chief Justice of the Supreme Court), and the more progressive wing, championed by figures like Senator Hiram Johnson of California.

The Old Guard favored limited government intervention in the economy, high tariffs to protect American industries, and a return to normalcy after the reformist zeal of the Progressive Era. They saw in Calvin Coolidge, who had ascended to the Presidency after Warren G. Harding's death in 1923, a leader who embodied their values.

The progressive wing, however, viewed Coolidge as overly cautious and beholden to big business. They yearned for a return to the progressive ideals of Theodore Roosevelt, advocating for greater regulation of corporations, social welfare programs, and a more active role for the United States on the world stage.

Their champion was Senator Robert La Follette of Wisconsin, a fiery orator and staunch progressive who would eventually challenge Coolidge as a third-party candidate.

The Convention Unfolds

The Republican National Convention, held from June 10th to 12th in Cleveland's Public Auditorium, was a tense affair from the outset. Coolidge, despite his incumbency, faced a surprisingly strong challenge from La Follette within the party ranks. The platform battles reflected the party's internal divisions, with heated debates over issues such as the League of Nations, farm relief, and Prohibition.

One of the most contentious issues was the Ku Klux Klan, which had experienced a resurgence in the 1920s and wielded significant influence in several states. While some Republicans condemned the Klan's racism and violence, others, particularly in the South, saw them as a potential source of votes. Ultimately, the convention adopted a platform that denounced "every endeavor to divide men in groups on the basis of religion or race," a carefully worded statement that, while not explicitly mentioning the Klan, was widely interpreted as a rebuke of the organization.

Coolidge Triumphant

Despite the internal divisions and challenges, the 1924 Republican National Convention ultimately served to solidify Calvin Coolidge's hold on the party. He secured the nomination on the first ballot, handily defeating La

Follette and other challengers. His running mate, former Budget Director Charles G. Dawes, further balanced the ticket, appealing to more conservative elements within the party.

Legacy and Impact

The 1924 Republican National Convention, though fraught with internal conflict, proved to be a significant turning point in American political history. It marked the beginning of the Republican Party's shift away from its progressive roots and towards a more conservative, pro-business stance, a trend that would continue throughout the 1920s and beyond.

Coolidge's victory in the general election, fueled in part by the deep divisions within the Democratic Party, solidified Republican control of the White House and ushered in an era of unprecedented economic prosperity, albeit one built on shaky foundations that would ultimately crumble with the Great Depression.

However, the convention also revealed the growing strength of progressive voices within the Republican Party and the deep divisions over issues like social welfare, economic inequality, and the role of government. These tensions, though temporarily subdued, would continue to simmer beneath the surface, eventually resurfacing with renewed vigor in the decades to come.

1928: Kansas City and the Coronation of "The Chief"

The summer of 1928 pulsed with an optimism unique to the Roaring Twenties. The Great War was a fading memory, the economy boomed, and flappers danced to the rhythm of jazz. Yet beneath the glittering surface, anxieties simmered. Prohibition fueled organized crime, xenophobia spurred immigration restrictions, and a cultural clash deepened between urban modernists and rural traditionalists. This complex tapestry formed the backdrop for the 1928 Republican National Convention, held in Kansas City, Missouri, a city embodying the era's contradictions.

Kansas City: Gateway to the West, Battleground of Change

Nestled at the confluence of the Missouri and Kansas Rivers, Kansas City was a city on the rise. Once a frontier outpost, it had blossomed into a bustling hub of agriculture, industry, and transportation. The iconic image of cowboys driving cattle through its stockyards competed with the burgeoning skyscrapers downtown. This blend of old and new, rural and urban, mirrored the nation at large, making it a fitting stage for the Republican Party's quest to maintain its grip on power.

The party itself was undergoing a transformation. The progressive wing, embodied by figures like Theodore Roosevelt, had waned, while a new conservatism, focused on business interests and limited government intervention, ascended. This shift was reflected in their chosen nominee, Herbert Hoover.

Hoover: The Engineer as President

Herbert Hoover, the Secretary of Commerce under the popular Calvin Coolidge, entered the convention as the clear frontrunner. His reputation as a brilliant engineer and efficient administrator, coupled with his success in managing relief efforts during World War I, made him a compelling figure. Hoover represented a new breed of technocratic leader, one who believed in the power of expertise and efficiency to solve the nation's problems.

But the convention wasn't merely a coronation. Issues like prohibition, religious prejudice (Hoover was Quaker, a rarity in national politics then), and agricultural relief animated the proceedings. The party platform, a document carefully crafted to appeal to a broad coalition, endorsed continued prohibition while acknowledging the need for farm relief, a nod to the growing discontent in the agricultural heartland.

The Spectacle and the Substance

Beyond the political maneuvering, the 1928 RNC showcased the evolving nature of American political conventions. Radio, still a relatively new medium, brought the speeches and debates into homes across the country. This expanded access helped shape public perception of the candidates and the issues, marking a turning point in how Americans experienced politics.

The convention hall buzzed with activity. Delegates, adorned with colorful banners and buttons proclaiming their state allegiance, engaged in fervent discussions. Journalists, eager to capture the drama and excitement, filed stories using the latest technology, including the newly invented telephoto lens.

A Legacy of Prosperity and its Limits

The 1928 RNC, in nominating Hoover and solidifying the Republican Party's platform, laid the groundwork for a landslide victory in the general election. However, the seeds of future turmoil were already sown. The emphasis on business interests and limited government intervention, while popular in the booming economy of 1928, would prove inadequate for addressing the challenges of the Great Depression, which began just a year later.

The convention in Kansas City serves as a reminder that even in moments of seeming triumph, the complexities of history are always at play. The decisions made in that grand hall, amidst the optimism and pageantry, would have a profound and lasting impact on the nation's trajectory, shaping the political landscape for decades to come.

1932: A Convention Shrouded in Gloom - Chicago's Soldier Field and the Weight of the Great Depression

The year 1932 saw the Republican National Convention descend upon Chicago, a city already grappling with the devastating realities of the Great Depression. Held within the colossal walls of Soldier Field, a stadium built to honor veterans of World War I, the convention ironically served as a stark reminder of a different kind of battle – the nation's struggle against economic ruin. While the "war to end all wars" was over, a different kind of conflict raged on: the fight to pull America out of the depths of despair.

A City and a Nation in Crisis

Chicago, known for its industrial prowess and bustling energy, bore the scars of the Depression. Unemployment lines snaked through the streets, breadlines became a lifeline for countless families, and the once vibrant city seemed to hold its breath, uncertain of the future. The selection of Soldier Field, a monument to past sacrifices, inadvertently underscored the immense challenges facing the present. The venue, capable of holding over 100,000 people, saw many of its seats empty, a testament to the economic hardship that gripped the nation.

The nation was in the throes of the Great Depression, triggered by the 1929 stock market crash. Unemployment soared above 20%, businesses shuttered, and millions faced poverty and hunger. The incumbent Republican President, Herbert Hoover, struggled to combat the crisis, his policies perceived as ineffective by a growing number of Americans. Hoover, once a symbol of American ingenuity and self-reliance, now represented, for many, the failures of the current system.

A Party Divided, a Nation Restless

Within the Republican Party, a palpable tension hung in the air. The party was grappling with its identity amidst the Depression. A faction led by Hoover clung to the belief in limited government intervention, advocating for individual initiative and volunteerism as the path out of the crisis. This approach, however, faced increasing criticism, perceived by many as out of touch with the dire reality faced by millions.

Opposing Hoover, though not directly challenging him for the nomination, were figures like former New York Governor Al Smith and Senator George Norris, who believed in a more proactive role for the government in addressing the economic calamity. They argued for increased public works projects, unemployment relief, and financial regulations to prevent future crises. This internal debate reflected the broader national conversation about the role of government in times of crisis.

The Inevitable Nomination and a Glimmer of Hope

Despite the undercurrent of dissent and the palpable sense of unease, President Hoover secured the Republican nomination for a second term. His acceptance speech, delivered at Soldier Field, reflected the somber mood of the nation. Acknowledging the hardships faced by millions, he defended his policies, emphasizing the importance of individual initiative and a balanced budget.

The 1932 Republican platform, however, offered a glimmer of hope for those seeking a more active response to the Depression. The platform acknowledged the need for federal relief efforts and endorsed public works projects as a means to create jobs. This shift, though subtle, reflected the party's recognition of the need to adapt to the changing needs of the nation.

The 1932 Republican National Convention, though overshadowed by the gloom of the Great Depression, marked a turning point in American history. The convention highlighted the internal divisions within the Republican Party regarding the role of government in addressing the crisis. It also signaled a subtle shift in the party's stance, acknowledging the need for a more proactive approach to tackling the economic challenges.

While Hoover would ultimately lose the 1932 election to Franklin Delano Roosevelt, the convention in Chicago foreshadowed the changing political landscape. The call for a more active government, though initially met with resistance by some within the Republican Party, would eventually pave the way for the New Deal and redefine the relationship between the American people and their government for decades to come. The 1932 convention, though held under the cloud of economic despair, ultimately served as a catalyst for change, forcing a reevaluation of long-held beliefs and paving the way for a new era in American politics.

1936: A Convention in the Shadow of the New Deal - Cleveland, Ohio

The year is 1936. The Great Depression, a specter that had haunted America for seven long years, cast a long shadow over the nation. Even as glimmers of hope emerged from the darkness, the wounds of economic hardship ran deep. In this climate of uncertainty and change, the Republican Party gathered in Cleveland, Ohio, to choose their standard-bearer for the upcoming presidential election. The 1936 Republican National Convention, held from June 9th to 12th, would prove to be a pivotal moment, not just for the party, but for the very course of American history.

Cleveland: A City Reeling, a Party Searching

Cleveland, a city synonymous with industrial might, was itself grappling with the harsh realities of the Depression. Unemployment was rampant, and labor unrest simmered beneath the surface. For the Republicans, choosing Cleveland as the host city was a strategic move, an attempt to reconnect with the working class who had, in large part, shifted their allegiance to Franklin Delano Roosevelt and the New Deal.

The Republican Party itself was at a crossroads. The crushing defeat of Herbert Hoover in 1932 had exposed deep divisions within its ranks. The old guard, clinging to the principles of laissez-faire economics and limited government, found themselves increasingly at odds with a growing progressive wing, who believed that the government had a role to play in addressing the social and economic ills plaguing the nation.

The Issues: Depression, Doubt, and the New Deal Divide

Dominating the convention were the issues born from the Depression and fueled by the New Deal. The Republicans found themselves on the defensive, forced to reckon with the immense popularity of Roosevelt's programs while trying to articulate a coherent alternative.

The New Deal, with its unprecedented government intervention in the economy, social security provisions, and large-scale public works projects, had fundamentally reshaped the political landscape. While many Republicans viewed it as anathema to their core principles, others recognized the need for a more compassionate and engaged government. This internal conflict played out on the convention floor, with heated debates over the role of government, social welfare, and the best path to economic recovery.

The Players: Landon Emerges from the Fray

The race for the Republican nomination was crowded and uncertain. Several prominent figures vied for the chance to challenge Roosevelt, including Senator Arthur Vandenberg of Michigan, known for his powerful oratory, and Senator Robert Taft of Ohio, a staunch conservative.

Yet, it was a relative newcomer, Governor Alf Landon of Kansas, who emerged as the compromise candidate. Landon, a fiscally conservative but socially moderate Republican, had gained national recognition for his balanced budget approach to governing Kansas during the Depression. While he opposed many aspects of the New Deal, he also recognized the need for some government intervention, particularly in the area of unemployment relief. This nuanced position, coupled with his reputation for honesty and integrity, made him an appealing choice for a party seeking to bridge its internal divides.

A Convention of Firsts: The Voice of the People Amplified

The 1936 Republican National Convention was not without its share of historical significance. It marked the first time that a major political convention was broadcast coast-to-coast on radio, bringing the political process directly into the homes of millions of Americans. This innovation would forever alter the dynamics of political conventions, transforming them into media spectacles with a far broader reach than ever before.

Adding to the drama was the surprising absence of the outgoing president, Herbert Hoover. This break from tradition, though attributed to illness at the time, underscored the shadow that Hoover's presidency, indelibly linked to the onset of the Depression, cast over the Republican Party.

Legacy: A Defining Moment, a Decisive Defeat

The 1936 Republican National Convention, despite its hopes for a resurgence, ultimately failed to unseat Roosevelt and his New Deal coalition. Landon's campaign, hampered by internal party divisions and the enduring popularity of Roosevelt, suffered a crushing defeat in the general election.

However, the convention was not without its long-term impact. It laid bare the deep fissures within the Republican Party, highlighting the ongoing struggle between its conservative and progressive wings, a battle that continues to shape the party to this day. Moreover, the convention's embrace of new technology, particularly radio, signaled a recognition of the growing importance of media and communication in American politics, a trend that would only accelerate in the decades to come.

The 1936 Republican National Convention in Cleveland serves as a potent reminder of a nation in flux, a political party grappling with its identity, and the enduring power of ideas in shaping the American story.

1940: A Philadelphia Story - Navigating Isolationism and Choosing a Challenger

The year 1940 saw the Republican National Convention descend upon the historic city of Philadelphia, Pennsylvania. The "City of Brotherly Love," steeped in the legacy of the nation's founding, provided a poignant backdrop for a party wrestling with its identity on the world stage and seeking a champion to challenge President Franklin Delano Roosevelt's bid for an unprecedented third term.

A World at War, America at a Crossroads

The specter of war loomed large over the convention. Across the Atlantic, Hitler's Germany had unleashed its blitzkrieg, conquering much of Europe and threatening the very foundations of democracy. The United States, however, remained deeply entrenched in isolationist sentiment. The wounds of World War I were still fresh, and a powerful contingent of Americans, particularly within the Republican Party, opposed any entanglement in foreign conflicts. This isolationist fervor was vividly illustrated by the formation of the America First Committee, a powerful lobby advocating against American intervention in the European war.

Domestically, the nation was still grappling with the lingering effects of the Great Depression. Though Roosevelt's New Deal programs had brought a measure of relief, unemployment remained high, and the economy was far from robust. Republicans campaigned on a platform of fiscal responsibility, criticizing the New Deal as excessive government intervention.

Leaders and Contenders: A Party Divided

The Republican Party in 1940 was a tapestry of differing ideologies. The "Old Guard," embodied by figures like former President Herbert Hoover, clung to traditional conservative principles of limited government and non-interventionism. However, a growing faction within the party, recognizing the global threat posed by the Axis powers, advocated for a more assertive foreign policy.

This divide was evident in the field of potential nominees. The early frontrunner was Senator Robert A. Taft of Ohio, a staunch isolationist and vocal critic of the New Deal. Taft represented the conservative wing of the party and enjoyed significant support from the

Republican establishment. Another prominent contender was Thomas E. Dewey, the young and charismatic District Attorney of New York, known for his successful prosecutions of organized crime. Dewey occupied a more moderate stance, advocating for preparedness and cautiously supporting aid to Great Britain.

Then there was Wendell Willkie, a dark horse candidate who had never held elected office. A former Democrat and a successful businessman, Willkie captivated the nation with his charisma, sharp intellect, and his vocal support for aiding the Allies against Nazi aggression. His outsider status and his compelling articulation of the threat posed by Hitler resonated with a public increasingly anxious about the war in Europe.

The Convention Unfolds: A Dark Horse Emerges

The 1940 Republican National Convention, held from June 24th to 28th, was a tense and dramatic affair. From the outset, it was clear that the party was deeply divided. The platform committee struggled to reconcile the isolationist stance favored by many delegates with the growing public sentiment for aiding the Allies. The resulting platform, a compromise crafted to appease both sides, lacked clarity and failed to offer a decisive vision for America's role in the world.

The nomination process itself was equally dramatic. Taft, the initial frontrunner, saw his support dwindle as the convention progressed. Dewey emerged as a strong contender, but his relative lack of experience counted against him. It was Willkie, however, who seized the moment. His electrifying speeches, delivered with conviction and passion, resonated with delegates and captivated the nation listening on the radio. He presented himself as a decisive leader, willing to confront the Nazi threat while also advocating for economic freedom and individual liberty.

As the balloting commenced, Willkie's momentum grew. By the sixth ballot, amidst a wave of support from delegates and a public clamoring for his nomination, Wendell Willkie secured the Republican nomination for President of the United States. His running mate was Senator Charles McNary of Oregon, a respected party elder who balanced Willkie's lack of experience in government.

The Legacy of 1940: A Turning Point for the GOP and the Nation

The 1940 Republican National Convention was a watershed moment, both for the Republican Party and for the nation. The nomination of Wendell Willkie, a political outsider who boldly challenged the isolationist orthodoxy within his own party, reflected a growing shift in public opinion towards engagement in the fight against fascism. While Willkie ultimately lost the election to Roosevelt, his campaign helped to galvanize public support for aiding the Allies. This paved the way for crucial policies like the Lend-Lease Act, which provided vital aid to Great Britain in its fight against Nazi Germany.

The 1940 convention also highlighted the enduring tensions within the Republican Party between its isolationist and interventionist wings. This debate, though muted during the unity of World War II, would re-emerge in the postwar years and continue to shape the party's foreign policy stances for decades to come. In many ways, the 1940 convention foreshadowed the future battles for the soul of the Republican Party, battles that continue to resonate in American politics today.

1944: A Nation at War, A Party Divided

Chicago in Wartime

The year is 1944. The world is embroiled in the deadliest conflict in human history. Against this backdrop of global struggle, the Republican Party convened in Chicago, Illinois, for its 22nd National Convention. The Windy City, a bustling hub of industry and commerce, was already deeply engaged in the war effort, its factories churning out tanks, planes, and munitions. The convention itself, held from June 26th to 28th at the Chicago Stadium, was a more subdued affair than in peacetime. The shadow of war loomed large, a constant reminder of the momentous decisions to be made not just by the Republican Party, but by the nation as a whole.

A World Ablaze, A Nation at the Crossroads

The defining issue of 1944 was undoubtedly World War II. By then, D-Day had just recently transpired, signaling a turning point in Europe, but the war in the Pacific raged on with brutal intensity. America was a nation fully mobilized, its young men and women fighting across the globe, its economy geared towards victory.

Domestic issues, while important, took a backseat to the overarching goal of defeating the Axis powers.

This wartime context deeply influenced the Republican National Convention. The party, traditionally associated with isolationism, found itself grappling with a new global reality. The question was not whether to be involved in the world but how.

Dewey vs. The Party: A Battle for the Soul of Republicanism

The fight for the Republican nomination in 1944 wasn't so much a contest as it was a coronation. Thomas E. Dewey, the energetic and ambitious governor of New York, had effectively sewn up the nomination long before the convention. Known for his successful prosecution of organized crime and his efficient, business-like approach to government, Dewey represented a new generation of Republican leadership.

However, the convention was not without its drama. Behind the scenes, a battle raged for the soul of the Republican Party. Dewey, though relatively moderate on most issues, faced opposition from the party's conservative wing. This faction, led by figures like Ohio Governor John W. Bricker, championed a more traditional Republican platform of limited government, fiscal conservatism, and a wary approach to international entanglements.

Bricker, chosen as Dewey's running mate in a bid for party unity, represented this internal struggle on the convention stage. His acceptance speech, in stark contrast to Dewey's, offered a more cautious vision for America's role in the postwar world. This internal division, however, was strategically downplayed during the convention itself. The party, acutely aware of the need for unity in a time of war, presented a united front to the American people.

Beyond the Nominees: Faces in the Crowd

Beyond the central figures of Dewey and Bricker, the 1944 RNC saw the rise of several figures who would go on to play significant roles in American politics. Among them was a young congressman from California named Richard Nixon, who delivered a rousing speech seconding Bricker's nomination for Vice President. This marked an early appearance on the national stage for a man who would go on to become both Vice President and President himself, though not without significant controversy.

Another notable figure was Earl Warren, then the Governor of California. Warren, a future Chief Justice of the Supreme Court, delivered the keynote address at the convention, a testament to his growing stature within the party. These rising stars, present at the convention alongside established leaders, underscored the generational shift occurring within the Republican Party.

A Legacy of Change and Continuity

The 1944 Republican National Convention, though overshadowed by the ongoing war, proved to be a significant event in the party's history. It marked the emergence of a new generation of Republican leaders, embodied by Dewey and those like Nixon who would follow in his footsteps. It also highlighted the internal divisions within the party between its moderate and conservative wings, a tension that would continue to shape Republican politics for decades to come.

Ultimately, Dewey and Bricker lost their bid for the White House to the incumbent Franklin D. Roosevelt and his running mate, Harry S. Truman. Yet, the 1944 convention laid the groundwork for the Republican Party's future. It began the process of redefining itself in a post-war world, moving away from isolationism and towards a more internationally engaged stance. The seeds sown in that Chicago stadium, amidst the uncertainty and anxiety of a world at war, would eventually blossom into the modern Republican Party.

1948: Crossroads at the Convention - Philadelphia's Battle for the Republican Soul

Philadelphia, the city of brotherly love, played host to a different kind of love affair in the summer of 1948: the Republican Party's enduring passion for power. Held in the cavernous Convention Hall, the 1948 Republican National Convention was anything but a predictable coronation. The nation, still basking in the afterglow of wartime victory, was grappling with the rising anxieties of the Cold War and the simmering tensions of social change. For the Republicans, the question wasn't just who would lead them against Truman and the Democrats, but what kind of party they wanted to be.

The Shadows of War and the Rise of a New World

The shadow of World War II loomed large over the convention. The global conflict had reshaped the political landscape, pushing issues like labor rights, economic regulation, and internationalism to the forefront. The burgeoning Cold War with the Soviet Union added another layer of complexity, demanding a firm hand on foreign policy and raising anxieties about communism at home.

The Republicans, out of power in the White House since 1933, sensed an opportunity. Yet, deep divisions plagued the party. The "Old Guard," represented by figures like Senator Robert Taft of Ohio, clung to a platform of small government, isolationism, and resistance to New Deal programs. Challenging this establishment were the "Modern Republicans," led by figures like Governor Thomas Dewey of New York and former Governor Harold Stassen of Minnesota. This faction embraced a more internationalist outlook and accepted a larger role for government in regulating the economy and providing social welfare.

The Leaders and their Legacies

Three figures dominated the contest for the Republican nomination:

- **Thomas E. Dewey:** The telegenic Governor of New York, Dewey projected an image of competence and efficiency. Having narrowly lost the 1944 presidential election to Franklin D. Roosevelt, he was seen by many as the frontrunner.
- **Robert A. Taft:** Known as "Mr. Republican," Taft was a staunch conservative and a powerful voice for isolationism. He commanded the loyalty of

the party's traditional base and was a formidable debater on issues like economic policy.

- **Harold Stassen:** A youthful and charismatic former Governor of Minnesota, Stassen represented the party's liberal wing. He campaigned on a platform of internationalism and social justice, advocating for civil rights advancements, a position that set him apart within the party.

Beyond these three, other contenders like Governor Earl Warren of California and Senator Arthur Vandenberg of Michigan added to the dynamism of the race, highlighting the diverse viewpoints vying for control of the Republican Party.

The Drama Unfolds: A Battle on the Convention Floor

The convention itself was a tense affair. The battle between the Old Guard and the Modern Republicans played out in debates over the party platform, particularly on civil rights and foreign policy. The platform committee, dominated by Taft supporters, sought to maintain the party's traditional stance on states' rights and limited government intervention in social issues. However, young Republicans, emboldened by the support of figures like Jackie Robinson, who had broken the color barrier in Major League Baseball that year, pushed for stronger language on civil rights.

The debate on foreign policy was equally heated. Stassen, a strong advocate for internationalism, challenged Taft's isolationist views. He advocated for a more active role for the United States in supporting war-torn Europe and containing Soviet expansion. Dewey, seeking to bridge the divide, positioned himself as a pragmatic leader capable of navigating the complexities of the postwar world.

Dewey's Triumph and the Missed Opportunity

After three ballots, Dewey emerged victorious, securing the Republican nomination for President. His running mate, Governor Earl Warren of California, brought further name recognition and balanced the ticket geographically.

While the outcome seemed to signal a victory for the Modern Republicans, the party remained deeply divided. The platform adopted at the convention was a compromise, reflecting the uneasy truce between the competing factions. This internal division would have significant consequences in the upcoming election.

Legacy of the 1948 RNC: A Defining Moment

The 1948 Republican National Convention was more than just a political event; it was a pivotal moment in the evolution of the Republican Party. It exposed the growing rift between the party's traditional base and a new generation of Republicans who embraced a more active role for government in addressing social and economic challenges.

While Dewey's subsequent defeat by President Truman in the general election solidified the Democrats' hold on the White House, the seeds of change had been sown. The debates over civil rights, foreign policy, and the role of government foreshadowed the ideological battles that would continue to shape the Republican Party for decades to come.

1952: The Showdown in Chicago

The year was 1952, and the Cold War cast a long, chilling shadow over America. The Korean War raged on, fueling anxieties about Communism's spread. At home, Senator Joseph McCarthy's fervent anti-communist crusade, though later deemed reckless and damaging, gripped the nation. This was the backdrop against which the Republican Party convened in Chicago for their 29th National Convention, eager to break a 20-year losing streak and reclaim the White House.

The Windy City Braces for a Political Storm

Chicago, known for its gritty industrial spirit and booming jazz scene, was no stranger to political drama. The city had hosted numerous conventions in the past, including the infamous 1948 Democratic National Convention, marred by protests and division. The 1952 Republican National Convention, held from July 7th to 11th at the International Amphitheatre, promised to be just as contentious, with deep divisions within the party itself.

A Nation Divided, a Party in Flux

Two major figures dominated the Republican landscape: the charismatic and controversial General Dwight D. Eisenhower, a war hero who transcended partisan lines, and Senator Robert A. Taft of Ohio, a staunch conservative and isolationist known as "Mr. Republican."

Taft, son of a former president, had long coveted the presidency and enjoyed considerable support from the party's conservative wing. He campaigned on a platform of limited government, fiscal responsibility, and a staunchly anti-communist stance. Eisenhower, on the other hand, represented a more moderate wing of the party. His lack of a clear political record prior to the convention, while disconcerting to some, also proved an advantage, allowing him to appeal to a broader spectrum of voters weary of partisan bickering.

The Battle for Hearts, Minds, and Delegates

The fight for the Republican nomination was fierce, playing out not just in public speeches and debates, but also in the backrooms of smoke-filled hotel suites. The convention itself was a spectacle of political maneuvering and high drama. Accusations of delegate tampering and rule manipulation flew between the Taft and Eisenhower camps. The controversy surrounding contested delegates, particularly from Texas, where questionable tactics were employed by both sides, became a defining issue of the convention.

"We Like Ike!" The General Takes the Stage

In a dramatic turn of events, the convention decided in favor of seating the pro-Eisenhower delegates, shifting the balance of power. This move effectively secured the nomination for Eisenhower, who accepted with a pledge to lead the nation to peace and prosperity. His running mate, the young and ambitious Senator Richard Nixon of California, balanced the ticket with his strong anti-communist credentials.

The energy inside the convention hall was electric as Eisenhower, radiating wartime leadership and genuine warmth, delivered a powerful acceptance speech. He spoke of the need for unity and a strong national defense, resonating with a nation grappling with Cold War anxieties. The chant "We Like Ike!" echoed through the hall and soon became a nationwide chorus.

1952 RNC: A Watershed Moment

The 1952 Republican National Convention was more than just a political event; it was a turning point for the Republican Party and the nation. It marked the rise of a new generation of Republican leadership embodied by Eisenhower, who went on to win the presidency in a landslide victory.

More significantly, the 1952 convention showcased the growing influence of television in American politics. For the first time, millions of Americans witnessed the drama of a national political convention unfold in their living rooms. This newfound access to the political process, with its inherent theatricality and behind-the-scenes glimpses, forever changed the way Americans engaged with their political system.

The legacy of the 1952 Republican National Convention is multifaceted. It ushered in a period of Republican dominance, shaped by Eisenhower's moderate conservatism and commitment to international engagement. It also highlighted the growing significance of television in shaping public opinion and political discourse. Most importantly, it revealed a nation eager for leadership, unity, and a path forward in a world increasingly defined by Cold War tensions.

1956: San Francisco and the Coronation of a War Hero

The year 1956 saw the Republican National Convention descend upon San Francisco, a city radiating Golden Gate optimism while grappling with the anxieties of a burgeoning Cold War. The Cow Palace, an expansive venue known more for livestock shows than political theater, played host to the Republican delegates. Despite the unconventional setting, the convention itself lacked any real sense of suspense. President Dwight D. Eisenhower, the revered war hero who had led the Allies to victory in Europe just a decade earlier, was a shoo-in for re-nomination.

A Nation at a Crossroads

The mid-1950s presented a complex tapestry of anxieties and aspirations for America. The Korean War had ended in a stalemate, leaving an undercurrent of unease about the spread of communism. McCarthyism, while on the wane, had sown seeds of suspicion and fear within American society. Yet, amidst this tension, a postwar economic boom was underway, fueling suburban growth and a burgeoning consumer culture.

Domestically, the Civil Rights Movement was steadily gaining momentum. The landmark Brown v. Board of Education decision of 1954 had declared school segregation unconstitutional, igniting a firestorm of resistance in the South and revealing deep racial divides within the nation.

Eisenhower's Steady Hand

Within this climate, Eisenhower projected an image of calm and experienced leadership. A moderate Republican, he had steered a middle course during his first term, avoiding the partisan battles that had characterized the Truman years. He oversaw the end of the Korean War, maintained a strong military posture against the Soviet Union, and presided over a period of economic prosperity.

His running mate, Vice President Richard Nixon, had weathered his own political storms. Accused of financial impropriety during the 1952 campaign, Nixon had salvaged his position with a heartfelt televised address, famously known as the "Checkers Speech." By 1956, Nixon had proven himself a loyal and effective lieutenant to Eisenhower.

A Unified Front, With Cracks Emerging

The 1956 RNC was a largely harmonious affair. Eisenhower's popularity was undeniable, and his re-nomination was never in doubt. However, beneath the surface of unity, fissures were beginning to emerge within the Republican Party.

The burgeoning conservative movement, though still largely marginalized within the party, found a voice in Ohio Senator Robert Taft. Taft, a staunch opponent of the New Deal and a critic of Eisenhower's moderate policies, had passed away in 1953. Yet, his conservative principles continued to resonate with a segment of the Republican base, particularly in the South and West, foreshadowing the ideological battles that would grip the party in the decades to come.

The Convention and Beyond

The 1956 RNC served primarily as a platform for Eisenhower to lay out his vision for a second term. In his acceptance speech, he emphasized themes of peace, prosperity, and progress. He warned against the dangers of communism abroad and pledged to maintain a strong national defense. Domestically, he promised to continue the economic growth of his first term and to address issues of education and healthcare.

While the convention itself may not have been a watershed moment in American history, it solidified Eisenhower's image as a unifying figure in a time of uncertainty. His resounding victory in the general election that year further cemented his legacy as a popular and effective leader. However, the seeds of change were already being sown. The 1956 RNC marked not only the coronation of a war hero but also the beginning of a gradual shift in the Republican Party, a shift that would ultimately reshape American politics in the decades to follow.

1960: A Convention of Contrasts in the City of Angels

Los Angeles Sets the Stage

The 1960 Republican National Convention, held in the shimmering heat of Los Angeles, California, from July 11th to 15th, was a study in contrasts. The location itself spoke volumes. Los Angeles, a city synonymous with Hollywood glamour and burgeoning industries, provided a stark contrast to the backdrop of the Cold War anxieties and social unrest simmering across the nation. The iconic Cocoanut Grove nightclub, the chosen venue for the convention, buzzed with the energy of political maneuvering, power brokering, and the anticipation of a nation on the brink of choosing its future.

A Nation at a Crossroads

The year 1960 marked the twilight of the Eisenhower era, a period characterized by post-war prosperity and a sense of stability. However, beneath the surface, the nation grappled with significant challenges. The Cold War with the Soviet Union cast a long shadow, fueled by events like the launch of Sputnik and growing concerns about communist influence. Domestically, the Civil Rights Movement was gaining momentum, challenging deeply ingrained racial segregation and inequality. The economy, while strong, was showing signs of sluggishness, raising concerns about the future.

The Leaders and Their Legacies

The Republican Party, seeking its third consecutive term in the White House, faced a pivotal moment. President Dwight D. Eisenhower, a towering figure whose popularity transcended party lines, was ineligible for re-election due to term limits. A new standard-bearer had to be chosen, one who could navigate the complex issues of the day and offer a compelling vision for the future.

The frontrunner was the sitting Vice President, Richard Nixon. A seasoned politician with a reputation for sharp intellect and aggressive campaigning, Nixon was seen as a natural successor to Eisenhower. However, he faced challenges from within his own party. Governor Nelson Rockefeller of New York, a liberal Republican, emerged as a vocal critic of Nixon's policies, particularly on social programs and civil rights. Senator Barry Goldwater of Arizona, a charismatic conservative, represented the burgeoning conservative wing of the party, advocating for smaller government and a more assertive foreign policy.

The Issues that Defined a Decade

The 1960 Republican National Convention became a battleground for these competing visions for the future of the party and the nation. The issue of civil rights, in particular, exposed deep divisions. The party platform adopted in Los Angeles reflected a compromise between the moderate and conservative factions. While it endorsed the Supreme Court's Brown v. Board of Education decision and called for equal opportunity, it stopped short of advocating for aggressive federal action to dismantle segregation. This cautious approach reflected the delicate balance the party was trying to strike between appealing to its base and attracting moderate voters.

The Cold War and its implications for foreign policy also took center stage. Nixon, capitalizing on his experience as Vice President, campaigned on a platform of strength and resolve against the Soviet Union. He emphasized his anti-communist credentials and pledged to maintain America's global leadership. Rockefeller and other moderates urged a more nuanced approach, advocating for diplomacy and engagement alongside military preparedness.

Drama and Intrigue Under the California Sun

Beyond the policy debates, the 1960 RNC was not without its share of drama and intrigue. One of the most memorable events unfolded not on the convention floor, but in a private meeting between Nixon and Rockefeller at the latter's suite in the Ambassador Hotel. The details of this encounter, later dubbed the "Compact of Fifth

Avenue," remain shrouded in some mystery, but it's widely believed that Rockefeller secured concessions from Nixon on policy issues, including civil rights, in exchange for withdrawing his candidacy and endorsing Nixon. This backroom deal highlighted the power dynamics and political maneuvering that often shaped the course of such events.

A Legacy of Change and Continuity

The 1960 Republican National Convention ultimately nominated Richard Nixon as its presidential candidate, with Henry Cabot Lodge Jr. as his running mate. While Nixon would lose a close and controversial election to John F. Kennedy, the convention set the stage for the future of the Republican Party. The conservative wing, energized by Goldwater's presence and message, would play an increasingly prominent role in party affairs, culminating in Goldwater's own nomination in 1964.

The 1960 RNC in Los Angeles served as a microcosm of a nation on the cusp of significant change. The issues debated, the compromises forged, and the personalities involved foreshadowed the turbulent yet transformative decade that lay ahead. While the Republicans ultimately fell short in their quest to retain the White House, the 1960 convention left an enduring mark on the party and American political history.

1964: A Conservative Earthquake in San Francisco

The year 1964 saw the Republican Party grappling with a fundamental identity crisis, played out on the national stage in the unlikely setting of San Francisco, California. While today the city is synonymous with liberalism, fifty years ago it hosted a Republican National Convention that reverberated with the anxieties of a nation on the cusp of radical change. The outcome of this convention, and the subsequent election, would shape not just the Republican Party's future, but the course of American politics for decades to come.

A City in Transition, A Party Divided

San Francisco in 1964 was a city teeming with contradictions. The burgeoning counterculture movement was beginning to take root, challenging traditional social norms and embracing free expression. Yet, this bastion of burgeoning liberalism was also chosen to host the Republican National Convention, highlighting the shifting political sands of the time.

The Republican Party itself was deeply fractured. The moderate wing, embodied by figures like New York Governor Nelson Rockefeller, favored a continuation of the progressive policies championed by President Eisenhower. However, a burgeoning conservative movement, fueled by anxieties over the Civil Rights Movement and the Cold War, saw the party's future in a starkly different light. This burgeoning conservative wing found its champion in Senator Barry Goldwater of Arizona.

Goldwater: A Harbinger of Change

Senator Barry Goldwater was a stark contrast to the Republican establishment. An ardent critic of big government, a staunch anti-communist, and a vocal opponent of the Civil Rights Act of 1964, Goldwater represented a clean break from the moderate Republicanism of the Eisenhower era. His fiery rhetoric and uncompromising stances resonated deeply with conservative activists, who saw in him a champion for their values.

The battle for the Republican nomination exposed the raw divisions within the party. Goldwater's supporters clashed repeatedly with those backing Rockefeller and other moderate candidates. The convention floor became a battleground for the soul of the Republican Party, with passionate arguments erupting over civil rights, the role of government, and the direction of the nation.

A Defining Moment: The Nomination of Goldwater

The climax of the convention came with Goldwater's acceptance speech. In a speech that would become a defining moment for both the Republican Party and the conservative movement, Goldwater declared: "Extremism in the defense of liberty is no vice. And let me remind you also that moderation in the pursuit of justice is no virtue." These words, met with thunderous applause from his supporters, sent shockwaves through the American political landscape.

Goldwater's nomination marked a significant shift to the right for the Republican Party. His candidacy energized conservative activists across the country, laying the groundwork for the rise of the "New Right" and the Reagan Revolution that would follow.

The Aftermath: A Lasting Legacy

While Goldwater ultimately lost the 1964 election in a landslide to Lyndon B. Johnson, his candidacy had a profound impact on American politics. His campaign galvanized conservative voters and helped to shift the Republican Party away from its moderate roots.

The 1964 Republican National Convention in San Francisco was a pivotal moment in American political history. It marked the ascendancy of conservatism within the Republican Party and laid the groundwork for the political realignment that would reshape American politics for decades to come. The echoes of Goldwater's uncompromising message continue to resonate within the Republican Party today, a testament to the enduring impact of that tumultuous convention in San Francisco.

1968: Miami Beach and the Year the Earth Moved

A Nation on the Brink

The year 1968 was a tumultuous one, etched in American memory for its social unrest and political upheaval. The Vietnam War raged on, casting a long shadow over the nation and fueling widespread protests. The assassinations of Martin Luther King Jr. and Robert F. Kennedy sent shockwaves through the country, exposing deep racial and political divisions. Cities burned in riots, reflecting the simmering anger over racial inequality and poverty.

It was against this backdrop of national crisis that Republicans gathered in Miami Beach, Florida, for their 1968 National Convention. The party, out of power since 1960, sensed an opportunity amidst the chaos, hoping to capitalize on the public's desire for law and order.

Sunshine and Shadow in Miami Beach

Miami Beach, known for its Art Deco architecture, glamorous nightlife, and pristine beaches, offered a stark contrast to the turmoil engulfing the nation. Yet, even this haven couldn't entirely escape the year's pervasive tension. Demonstrators, largely focused on the Vietnam War, gathered outside the convention hall, their chants and placards a constant reminder of the nation's divided soul.

The Contenders and the Issues

The race for the Republican nomination was fiercely contested. Richard Nixon, the party's standard-bearer in the 1960 defeat, emerged as the frontrunner. His experience, name recognition, and carefully crafted image of a seasoned statesman resonated with a public yearning for stability. His main rivals included the liberal Governor Nelson Rockefeller of New York and the staunch conservative Governor Ronald Reagan of California.

The issues dominating the convention reflected the nation's anxieties. The Vietnam War was paramount, with Republicans debating the best course of action. Nixon campaigned on a platform of "peace with honor," a vague promise that appealed to those weary of the war but unwilling to accept defeat.

The economy, particularly rising inflation, was another key concern. Law and order emerged as a central theme, a response to the year's riots and protests. Nixon, with his tough-on-crime rhetoric, skillfully tapped into the public's anxieties, promising to restore order and stability.

The Rise of the "Southern Strategy"

The 1968 RNC is also notable for the solidification of the "Southern Strategy," a tactic that would profoundly reshape American politics. Recognizing the shifting political landscape in the South, where white voters were increasingly disillusioned with the Democratic Party's embrace of civil rights, Nixon made a calculated appeal to racial resentment. While he avoided explicitly racist language, his emphasis on "law and order," "states' rights," and opposition to forced busing resonated with white Southerners anxious about the pace of social change.

A Convention of Firsts and Lasts

The 1968 RNC was marked by several notable events:

- **The first televised convention in color:** This technological advancement brought the spectacle and drama of the convention into American living rooms like never before, highlighting the growing power of television in shaping political perceptions.

- **The decline of party bosses:** Nixon's nomination victory signaled a shift away from the traditional backroom deals and power brokers who had long dominated the nominating process. His successful use of television and direct appeals to voters marked the growing influence of mass media and the rise of candidate-centered campaigns.

- **The emergence of Spiro Agnew:** Nixon's selection of Spiro Agnew, the relatively unknown Governor of Maryland, as his running mate surprised many. Agnew, with his sharp tongue and willingness to attack the media and liberals, quickly became a polarizing figure. His selection demonstrated Nixon's intention to aggressively court disaffected white voters.

The Legacy of 1968

The 1968 Republican National Convention was more than just a political event; it was a microcosm of a nation grappling with profound challenges and undergoing a period of seismic change. The convention solidified Nixon's hold on the Republican Party and propelled him to the presidency. However, the divisions exposed and exploited during the campaign, particularly on race and the war in Vietnam, continued to shape American politics for decades to come. The "Southern Strategy," born in the shadow of Miami Beach's shimmering facade, helped reshape the political landscape, contributing to the realignment of the two major parties and leaving a lasting impact on American democracy.

1972: Miami Beach and the Dawn of Southern Strategy

The shimmering heat of Miami Beach, Florida, set the stage for the 1972 Republican National Convention. Held from August 21st to 23rd at the Miami Beach Convention Center, the convention saw the renomination of incumbent President Richard Nixon and Vice President Spiro Agnew. While seemingly a straightforward affair, with Nixon sailing to victory in the general election, the 1972 RNC provides a window into a pivotal period in American political history, marked by social change, political realignment, and the solidifying of the "Southern Strategy" within the Republican Party.

A Nation in Flux

The backdrop for the 1972 election was one of significant domestic and international tension. The Vietnam War continued to rage, casting a long shadow over American society. The anti-war movement remained vocal, fueling a sense of national division. Economically, the nation grappled with inflation, a consequence of the war and other factors, further contributing to a feeling of unease.

137

Socially, the Civil Rights Movement had spurred significant progress, but racial tensions remained high. The push for equal rights for women was also gaining momentum, sparking debate and dividing traditionalists and progressives. These issues, along with anxieties about crime and urban decay, created fertile ground for political change.

The Rise of Nixon and the Southern Strategy

Richard Nixon, a seasoned politician with a complex legacy, expertly navigated this tumultuous landscape. Having lost narrowly to John F. Kennedy in 1960, Nixon had rebuilt his image, appealing to a "silent majority" he believed yearned for stability and a return to traditional values.

Central to Nixon's strategy was the cultivation of white Southern voters, a demographic traditionally aligned with the Democratic Party. This approach, dubbed the "Southern Strategy," involved appealing to racial anxieties and resentment towards the Civil Rights Movement, often through coded language and appeals to "law and order." While the term itself was coined later, the 1972 RNC saw the strategy solidify, marking a significant realignment in American politics with long-lasting consequences.

The Convention and its Players

The 1972 RNC itself was a carefully orchestrated affair. Nixon, with his commanding lead in the polls, faced no serious opposition within the party. The convention served primarily as a platform to solidify his image, promote his "law and order" message, and launch his re-election campaign.

Key figures within the Republican Party rallied around Nixon. Vice President Spiro Agnew, known for his fiery rhetoric and attacks on the media and the left, remained a loyal and powerful voice. Other prominent figures included future President Ronald Reagan, then Governor of California, and Senator Barry Goldwater of Arizona, the conservative icon who had lost decisively to Lyndon B. Johnson in 1964.

While the convention lacked any real drama in terms of nominee selection, it did witness protests and demonstrations, primarily from anti-war activists. These demonstrations, though largely peaceful, highlighted the deep divisions within American society at the time.

Lasting Impacts and the Legacy of '72

The 1972 RNC and the subsequent election of Richard Nixon to a second term had profound implications for American political history. The solidifying of the Southern Strategy within the Republican Party helped reshape the nation's political landscape, contributing to the decline of the "Solid South" for Democrats and the rise of a more conservative Republican Party.

Furthermore, the convention highlighted the effectiveness of Nixon's appeal to the "silent majority," a strategy that resonated with voters weary of social unrest and yearning for stability. This approach, with its focus on cultural anxieties and anxieties over social change, continues to echo in American politics today.

However, the triumph of 1972 would be short-lived for Nixon and the Republican Party. The Watergate scandal, which began as a seemingly minor break-in at the Democratic National Committee headquarters, would unravel Nixon's presidency, forcing his resignation in 1974. The scandal cast a long shadow over American politics, eroding public trust and fueling cynicism towards government.

In conclusion, the 1972 Republican National Convention, seemingly a straightforward event in a year dominated by Richard Nixon's re-election, holds a more complex and significant place in history. It marked a turning point in American politics, highlighting the effectiveness of the Southern Strategy, the anxieties of a nation grappling with change, and the enduring legacy of a President who would both reshape American politics and ultimately be brought down by his own ambition.

1976: A Convention of Unknowns and Upsets in Kansas City

The year is 1976. The United States, still reeling from the Watergate scandal and a humiliating withdrawal from Vietnam, prepares to elect its next leader. For Republicans, the upcoming election presented both a challenge and an opportunity. The challenge was to reclaim the White House after four years of Democrat Jimmy Carter's presidency. The opportunity lay in capitalizing on the nation's disillusionment and offering a fresh, conservative vision for the future. The stage for this political drama was set in the heartland of America, Kansas City, Missouri, host to the 1976 Republican National Convention.

Kansas City: The Heart of America Plays Host

Kansas City, known for its jazz heritage and succulent barbecue, was an unusual, but strategic choice. By selecting a city in the Midwest, the Republican Party aimed to distance itself from the scandals of Washington D.C. and appeal to the "silent majority" - the working and middle-class Americans who felt ignored by the perceived liberal elites. The city, eager to showcase its revitalized downtown, pulled out all the stops, offering delegates and attendees a taste of Midwestern hospitality amidst the high-stakes political maneuvering.

A Nation in Flux

The shadow of Watergate loomed large over the nation. The resignation of President Richard Nixon in 1974 had left a deep scar on the Republican Party, leading to a loss of public trust and a surge in Democratic support. The economy, grappling with stagflation (a combination of high inflation and unemployment), added to the national unease. The Vietnam War, though officially over, continued to cast a long shadow, with lingering questions about America's role in the world and the treatment of returning veterans.

The Players on the National Stage

The race for the Republican nomination was wide open. President Gerald Ford, who had assumed office after Nixon's resignation, faced a formidable challenge from the charismatic former California Governor Ronald Reagan. Ford, representing the establishment wing of the party, campaigned on a platform of stability and experience. Reagan, on the other hand, energized the conservative base with his calls for smaller government, lower taxes, and a strong national defense.

Other prominent figures at the convention included:

- **Bob Dole:** The Kansas Senator, known for his sharp wit and legislative acumen, served as Ford's running mate.

- **Howard Baker:** The Tennessee Senator, who gained national prominence during the Watergate hearings, delivered the keynote address, emphasizing the need for the party to rebuild trust with the American people.

- **Anne Armstrong:** The former U.S. Ambassador to the United Kingdom, played a pivotal role in advocating for women's rights within the party and became the first woman to place a name in nomination for President at a Republican National Convention.

A Convention of Twists and Turns

The 1976 Republican National Convention was anything but predictable. The first ballot resulted in a narrow victory for Ford, but he fell short of securing the nomination outright. A dramatic fight for delegates ensued, with both campaigns working tirelessly to sway undecided votes. The tension reached a fever pitch as the convention headed towards a second ballot.

Legacy of an Upset

In the end, Gerald Ford secured the nomination, choosing Bob Dole as his running mate. However, the convention's legacy went beyond the final vote count. The close contest and the fervent support for Reagan signaled a growing conservative movement within the

Republican Party, one that would ultimately reshape the political landscape.

The 1976 Republican National Convention in Kansas City marked a turning point in American political history. It showcased a party grappling with its past, seeking to redefine itself amidst a nation yearning for change. While Ford would lose the general election to Jimmy Carter, the seeds of a conservative resurgence were sown, setting the stage for Ronald Reagan's landslide victory four years later. The convention, held in the heartland of America, reflected the changing tides of American politics, signaling a shift towards conservative values and setting the stage for a new era in American political history.

1980: A Detroit Rebirth for the Republican Party

The Motor City Shifts Gears

The year was 1980. A palpable sense of disillusionment hung in the air across America. The once shimmering promise of the American Dream felt tarnished. Inflation was rampant, unemployment stubbornly high, and the nation grappled with an energy crisis. In the midst of this national unease, Detroit, the Motor City, hosted the 1980 Republican National Convention, hoping to showcase a city battling back from economic hardship and racial tension.

The choice of Detroit as the host city was strategic. It represented the heartland of American industry, a sector struggling to remain competitive on the world stage. The Republican Party, under the leadership of Chairman Bill Brock, saw an opportunity to connect with blue-collar workers traditionally aligned with the Democratic Party, many of whom felt abandoned by the perceived failures of the Carter administration.

A Nation at a Crossroads

The political landscape in 1980 was dominated by a sense of national malaise. The Iran Hostage Crisis continued to unfold, casting a dark shadow over President Jimmy Carter's presidency. Adding to the national anxieties, the Cold War with the Soviet Union continued with no end in sight. Americans yearned for a strong leader who could restore their faith in the nation and navigate these complex global challenges.

The Republican Party itself was at a turning point. The moderate wing, represented by figures like George H.W. Bush, was challenged by a surging conservative movement, energized by the candidacy of Ronald Reagan. This internal struggle for the soul of the Republican Party played out vividly at the convention.

Reagan's Ascent and a Party Transformed

Ronald Reagan, the former governor of California, entered the convention as the clear front-runner. His message of optimism, smaller government, and a strong national defense resonated with many Americans disillusioned by the status quo. Yet, his nomination was not a foregone conclusion. George H.W. Bush and his supporters fought hard, hoping to sway delegates with a more moderate, establishment approach.

The convention witnessed a dramatic moment that would shape the future of the Republican Party. Reagan, in a surprising move, selected George H.W. Bush as his running mate. This bold decision served to unify the party, bringing together the conservative and moderate factions under a single ticket. It also signaled a shift in Republican politics, marking the rising influence of conservative ideology within the party.

Beyond the Ballot: Stories from the Convention Floor

Beyond the political maneuvering and speeches, the 1980 RNC was also a stage for compelling human stories. The convention hall buzzed with the energy of delegates from across the country, each carrying their hopes and anxieties for the future. The presence of prominent African American Republicans, like Congressman Jack Kemp, highlighted the party's efforts to broaden its appeal beyond its traditional base.

One of the most enduring images from the convention is the sight of Reagan and his wife, Nancy, beaming with optimism as balloons fell from the rafters. The image captured the hope and energy that Reagan projected, a stark contrast to the perceived gloom of the Carter years.

The Legacy of 1980: A Turning Point in American Politics

The 1980 Republican National Convention was more than just a political event; it was a turning point in American history. The convention showcased a nation grappling with economic uncertainty and international challenges, searching for a new direction. It marked the ascendance of Ronald Reagan and the rise of conservatism as a powerful force in American politics. Reagan's message of optimism and his promise to restore American pride resonated deeply with voters. The policies enacted during his presidency, often referred to as the "Reagan Revolution," continue to shape American politics and society to this day. The 1980 RNC, held in the heart of a struggling Detroit, became the launchpad for a new era in American political history.

1984: Dallas and the Dawn of the Reagan Revolution, Part II

A City of Dreams and Discontent

The 1984 Republican National Convention, held in Dallas, Texas from August 20th to 23rd, pulsed with an air of triumphalism. The city, synonymous with oil wealth, cowboy bravado, and the tragic assassination of John F. Kennedy two decades prior, seemed a fitting backdrop for Ronald Reagan's bid for a second term. Dallas, in 1984, was a city grappling with its own identity – a microcosm of the national mood caught between the lingering shadows of the past and the dazzling promise of a future championed by Reagan.

Morning in America, Shadows of the Cold War

The nation, in 1984, was riding a wave of economic optimism fueled by Reagan's supply-side economics. "Morning in America," the iconic phrase from Reagan's re-election campaign ads, resonated with many Americans experiencing renewed prosperity. However, this bright facade was juxtaposed against the ever-present chill of the Cold War. The Soviet Union, under the new leadership of Mikhail Gorbachev, remained a formidable adversary, and the nuclear arms race cast a long shadow over the world.

Domestically, while Reagan preached smaller government, social issues like abortion, affirmative action, and the burgeoning AIDS crisis sparked heated debates, revealing deep fissures within the American fabric. The Democratic Party, still reeling from their 1980 defeat, sought to position themselves as the party of the working class, challenging Reagan's economic policies. Their nominee, former Vice President Walter Mondale, and his running mate, Geraldine Ferraro, the first woman on a major party ticket, aimed to offer a stark alternative to Reagan's vision.

Reagan's Republican Party: A New Coalition

The Republican Party, under Reagan's leadership, had undergone a significant transformation. Reagan, once considered too conservative by the Republican establishment, had successfully forged a new coalition by attracting disaffected Democrats, evangelical Christians, and blue-collar workers concerned about the economy. This "Reagan Democrat" phenomenon fundamentally reshaped the political landscape, solidifying the conservative shift within the Republican Party and laying the groundwork for its future dominance.

Key figures in the Reagan administration and the Republican Party, like Vice President George H.W. Bush, future Secretary of State James Baker, and the rising star, Jack Kemp, played crucial roles in solidifying Reagan's re-election campaign. The 1984 convention saw the party rally around their charismatic leader, presenting a united front and a clear message of optimism and strength.

A Coronation, Not a Convention

The 1984 Republican National Convention was, in essence, a coronation rather than a contest. Reagan faced no serious opposition and sailed to a resounding first-ballot nomination. His acceptance speech, delivered against a backdrop of American flags and fervent supporters, encapsulated the prevailing mood of the convention and the country. He spoke of America as a "shining city on a hill," a beacon of freedom and opportunity.

Echoes of the Convention

The 1984 Republican National Convention solidified Reagan's image as a transformative figure in American politics. His landslide victory in the general election that year, securing 49 states, was a testament to his enduring popularity and the effectiveness of his message.

However, beyond the jubilation, the convention also foreshadowed the future trajectory of the Republican Party. The seeds of the "culture wars," the increasing influence of social conservatism, and the embrace of a more assertive foreign policy, all of which would come to define the party in the decades to come, were already evident in the Dallas heat of August 1984.

While "Morning in America" was the dominant narrative, the 1984 RNC also highlighted the growing sociopolitical divisions within the nation – divisions that continue to resonate today. In many ways, the legacy of the 1984 Republican National Convention is not just about the triumph of Ronald Reagan, but also about the crystallization of a new political order and the beginning of a new chapter in the American story.

New Orleans and the Anointing of a Successor - 1988

The Superdome, New Orleans, Louisiana. August 1988. The air crackled with a strange mix of humidity, Dixieland jazz, and political ambition. This wasn't just another Republican National Convention; it was the culmination of a decade defined by Reaganism, and the party faithful were gathered to crown their champion for the upcoming election.

A Nation on the Cusp of Change

The historical context of the 1988 RNC was one of transition. The Cold War, the defining geopolitical struggle for a generation, was thawing, with President Ronald Reagan and Soviet Premier Mikhail Gorbachev having signed the landmark INF Treaty the previous year. The American economy, while enjoying a period of growth, was grappling with issues like a growing deficit and income inequality. The social fabric, meanwhile, was strained by debates over abortion, the AIDS crisis, and the War on Drugs.

153

The Gipper's Shadow Looms Large

Reagan, nearing the end of his second term, loomed large over the convention, his presence felt even in absentia. The Republican Party was his party now, shaped by his conservative ideology and charismatic leadership. The question wasn't so much about policy, as it was about finding the candidate who could best embody the Reagan legacy.

The Contenders: A Vice President and a Maverick

The frontrunner was the incumbent Vice President, George H.W. Bush. Experienced, steady, but lacking Reagan's charisma, Bush represented a continuation of the status quo. His main challenger, though not initially seen as a serious threat, was the charismatic but controversial televangelist, Pat Robertson. Robertson energized the social conservative wing of the party, tapping into anxieties about cultural change and religious freedom.

The Big Easy Sets the Stage

New Orleans, with its unique blend of cultures, music, and history, provided a vibrant backdrop for the convention. The city, still recovering from the economic downturn of the early 80s, welcomed the influx of delegates and media, showcasing its resilience and spirit. However, the choice of New Orleans also highlighted the ongoing struggle for racial equality, with some questioning the GOP's commitment to civil rights.

"Read My Lips: No New Taxes"

One of the most memorable moments of the 1988 RNC came during Bush's acceptance speech. Seeking to differentiate himself from his Democratic opponent, Michael Dukakis, and appeal to a nation wary of tax hikes, Bush uttered the now-famous line: "Read my lips: No new taxes." This pledge, while powerful in the moment, would come back to haunt him during his presidency.

A More Inclusive Party Image?

The 1988 RNC saw a concerted effort by the Republican Party to broaden its appeal. The party showcased a more diverse group of speakers and highlighted issues like education and drug policy, aiming to attract women and minority voters. This effort, though nascent, marked the beginning of a long-term strategy to reshape the party's image.

The Legacy of the 1988 RNC

The 1988 Republican National Convention successfully anointed George H.W. Bush as the heir to the Reagan legacy. The party emerged seemingly unified, with a clear message of economic prosperity and conservative values. Bush would go on to win the general election, defeating Dukakis.

However, the seeds of future divisions were already present. The social conservatism that propelled Robertson's candidacy would continue to grow within the party, while the promise of "no new taxes" would prove difficult to keep, ultimately contributing to Bush's defeat in 1992.

The 1988 RNC, therefore, stands as a pivotal moment in American political history – a time of transition and transformation for the Republican Party, and for the nation as a whole. It marked the end of an era defined by Reagan, and the beginning of a new chapter, one whose consequences are still being felt today.

1992: Houston, We Have a (Culture) War

The Astrodome, Houston, Texas. August 17-20, 1992. The city known for space exploration found itself hosting a different kind of frontier: a Republican Party grappling with its identity after twelve years out of the White House and facing a rapidly changing world. The 1992 Republican National Convention, more than just nominating George H.W. Bush for a second term, laid bare the cultural and political fault lines that would continue to define American politics for decades to come.

The Backdrop: Recession and the End of the Cold War

The Berlin Wall had fallen, the Soviet Union dissolved, and the Cold War, the defining conflict of a generation, was over. Yet, victory felt bittersweet for many Americans. The economy, mired in recession, overshadowed the triumph over communism. Unemployment hovered above 7%, and President Bush, once lauded for his foreign policy prowess, faced criticism for his handling of domestic issues. The Democratic challenger, Arkansas Governor Bill Clinton, successfully tapped into the economic anxieties of the electorate, famously campaigning on the slogan, "It's the economy, stupid."

The Party Divided: Moderates vs. Social Conservatives

The Republican Party in 1992 was a house divided. On one side stood the pragmatic, moderate wing, epitomized by President Bush and his allies. This faction prioritized fiscal conservatism, free trade, and a less interventionist foreign policy. On the other side, a burgeoning social conservative movement, fueled by concerns over abortion, gay rights, and secularism in public life, sought to pull the party further to the right.

This internal struggle came to a head during the convention. Pat Buchanan, a conservative commentator and former Nixon speechwriter, challenged Bush in the primaries, galvanizing the social conservative base with his fiery rhetoric. Although unsuccessful in unseating the incumbent, Buchanan's influence on the party platform and the tone of the convention was undeniable.

"A Cultural War for the Soul of America"

Buchanan's address to the convention, dubbed the "culture war" speech, became the most memorable and controversial moment of the event. He painted a stark picture of America divided between two conflicting visions: a "religious war going on in our country for the soul of America," pitting traditional values against a liberal, secular agenda.

While Bush attempted to distance himself from the divisive tone, the speech energized the conservative base and highlighted the growing influence of social issues within the Republican Party. It signaled a shift away from the pragmatic conservatism of Reagan and the first Bush presidency towards a more ideological and culturally focused brand of conservatism.

The Players: Familiar Faces and Rising Stars

Beyond Bush and Buchanan, the 1992 RNC featured a cast of characters who would go on to shape American politics in the years to come. Vice President Dan Quayle, battling perceptions of inexperience, delivered a forceful defense of the administration's record. A young, relatively unknown governor from Texas named George W. Bush introduced his father to the delegates, offering a glimpse of the future of the Republican Party.

On the Democratic side, Bill Clinton and his running mate, Senator Al Gore, watched the unfolding drama in Houston with keen interest. The Republican focus on social issues, while mobilizing their base, also risked alienating moderate voters—a dynamic the Clinton campaign expertly exploited in the general election.

The Legacy: A Turning Point for the GOP

The 1992 Republican National Convention was more than just a political event—it was a cultural signpost. It marked the ascendency of social conservatism as a driving force within the Republican Party, a trend that continues to this day.

The "culture war" speech, though controversial, resonated with a segment of the population who felt that their values were under attack in a rapidly changing society. This sentiment, tapped into by subsequent Republican leaders, would become a powerful mobilizing force in American politics.

The 1992 RNC, while ultimately unsuccessful in securing a second term for President Bush, laid the groundwork for the future direction of the Republican Party. It highlighted the tensions within the party between its moderate and conservative wings, a dynamic that continues to shape its identity and electoral strategies. In the grand narrative of American political history, the 1992 convention stands as a pivotal chapter, marking the beginning of a new era of cultural and political polarization.

1996: San Diego's Sunshine and the Promise of a Bridge to the Future

The year was 1996. The Cold War was a fading memory, replaced by the burgeoning anxieties and opportunities of globalization and the internet age. Bill Clinton, the charismatic Democrat, was finishing his first term, having ridden the wave of economic prosperity and a more centrist image to defeat incumbent George H.W. Bush four years prior. The Republicans, eager to reclaim the White House, descended upon sunny San Diego, California, for their 1996 Republican National Convention.

Setting the Stage: San Diego and the Political Landscape

San Diego, with its idyllic coastline and laid-back atmosphere, provided a stark contrast to the intense political drama about to unfold. The city, known for its strong military presence, was also becoming a hub for

161

technology and innovation, reflecting the changing face of America.

The Republican Party itself was at a crossroads. The shadow of the Reagan Revolution still loomed large, but the rise of Newt Gingrich and the "Republican Revolution" of 1994, which handed control of Congress to the GOP for the first time in decades, signaled a shift towards a more confrontational, conservative approach.

The Issues: A Nation in Transition

The 1996 election, and by extension the RNC, grappled with the anxieties and aspirations of a nation in flux. The economy, while strong, was undergoing a period of rapid technological advancement that left many feeling left behind. Globalization, while opening new markets, also fueled fears of job losses and cultural change.

Against this backdrop, key issues debated at the convention included:

- **The Economy:** Republicans argued for tax cuts, deregulation, and a balanced budget, echoing the supply-side economics of the Reagan era. They aimed to contrast their vision with Clinton's more interventionist approach.
- **Welfare Reform:** Welfare reform was a hot-button issue, with Republicans pushing for stricter work requirements and limitations on benefits, framing it as a way to promote personal responsibility and reduce government dependency.

- **Family Values:** Social issues, particularly abortion and gay rights, continued to be major points of contention. The party platform reflected the socially conservative values of the Republican base.
- **The Role of Government:** The debate over the size and scope of government remained central. Republicans advocated for devolution of power to the states, echoing the anti-federalist sentiments gaining traction within the party.

The Players: Dole vs. Clinton, a Study in Contrasts

The 1996 RNC officially nominated Senator Bob Dole from Kansas as the Republican presidential candidate. A World War II veteran and respected legislator, Dole represented a more moderate, pragmatic wing of the party. His running mate, Jack Kemp, former congressman and housing secretary under President George H.W. Bush, brought economic expertise and a more optimistic, inclusive message.

Facing an uphill battle against the popular incumbent, Dole struggled to galvanize the electorate. Clinton, skillfully navigating the political center, painted Dole as an out-of-touch relic of the past, while portraying himself as the best steward for a nation entering a new millennium.

Illustrious Moments and Lasting Impact

Several key moments punctuated the 1996 RNC:

- **Colin Powell's Speech:** The highly respected former Chairman of the Joint Chiefs of Staff, Colin Powell, delivered a powerful address emphasizing his moderate views and implicitly criticizing the more extreme elements of the party.
- **The Promise of a "Bridge to the Future":** Dole attempted to bridge the generational gap, presenting himself as a seasoned leader who could guide the country into the 21st century, while still upholding traditional values.
- **The Rise of the Religious Right:** The influence of the religious right within the Republican Party was undeniable, shaping the party platform and highlighting the growing role of social issues in American politics.

The 1996 RNC ultimately failed to produce a winning formula for the Republicans. Dole's campaign struggled to gain traction, and Clinton secured a comfortable victory in both the popular vote and the electoral college.

However, the convention laid bare the internal divisions and evolving identity of the Republican Party. The tensions between moderate and conservative factions, the growing influence of the religious right, and the party's struggle to appeal to a changing electorate foreshadowed the challenges and transformations that lay ahead. The 1996 RNC serves as a reminder of a nation grappling with its identity at the dawn of a new era, and a political party searching for its place in a rapidly evolving world.

Philadelphia, 2000 - A "Compassionate Conservative" in the Cradle of Liberty

The year 2000 marked a pivotal moment in American history. The 20th century was ending, and a new millennium was dawning, bringing with it a sense of both excitement and uncertainty. The nation was experiencing an economic boom, yet social anxieties lingered. It was against this backdrop that the Republican Party chose Philadelphia, the city where the Declaration of Independence was signed and the Constitution drafted, as the stage for their national convention.

The Setting and the Stakes

Philadelphia, steeped in history and symbolism, provided a resonant backdrop for the Republican narrative. By convening in the "Cradle of Liberty," the GOP aimed to connect themselves to the nation's founding ideals and project an image of stability and traditional values.

The stakes were high. After eight years under Democratic President Bill Clinton, the Republicans were eager to reclaim the White House. The party saw an opportunity in the public's desire for a change from the scandals that had plagued the Clinton administration, even if the economy was thriving.

The Issues that Defined the Moment

Several key issues dominated the national conversation in 2000, shaping the political landscape and influencing the Republican platform.

- **The Economy and the Tech Boom:** The dot-com bubble was at its peak, fueling unprecedented economic growth. The Republicans, traditionally aligned with pro-business policies, aimed to capitalize on this prosperity by promising continued economic growth and tax relief.
- **Education Reform:** Education reform was emerging as a major concern, with debates surrounding school choice and standardized testing taking center stage. The Republicans

championed school choice initiatives and advocated for higher standards in education.

- **Moral and Social Values:** Social issues, particularly abortion and same-sex marriage, remained deeply divisive. The Republican Party, reflecting its conservative base, emphasized its commitment to "family values" and took a strong stance against abortion and same-sex marriage.

The Key Players

The 2000 Republican National Convention saw a confluence of established party leaders and rising stars, all vying to shape the party's future:

- **George W. Bush:** The Governor of Texas and son of former President George H.W. Bush, George W. Bush, emerged as the party's nominee. His campaign focused on "compassionate conservatism," emphasizing a more inclusive image while upholding traditional Republican values.

- **Dick Cheney:** The seasoned politician and former Secretary of Defense under George H.W. Bush was chosen by George W. Bush as his running mate. Cheney's experience and gravitas brought a sense of stability and expertise to the ticket.

- **Colin Powell:** The highly respected retired four-star general and former Chairman of the Joint Chiefs of Staff delivered a powerful speech at the convention. Although a moderate Republican,

Powell's endorsement of Bush carried significant weight and broadened the candidate's appeal.

- **John McCain:** The Arizona Senator and former Vietnam War hero, who had lost a hard-fought primary battle against Bush, played a crucial role in unifying the party. His presence at the convention and endorsement of Bush demonstrated a commitment to party unity.

Illustrious Moments and Lasting Impact

The 2000 Republican National Convention was marked by several key events and speeches that left a lasting impact:

- **The Theme of "Compassionate Conservatism":** This defining theme of George W. Bush's campaign aimed to soften the edges of traditional conservatism, presenting a more inclusive and empathetic approach to social issues. While critics questioned its sincerity, it proved to be an effective strategy in attracting moderate voters.

- **Laura Bush's Speech:** In a departure from tradition, Laura Bush, a former librarian known for her reserved demeanor, delivered a well-received speech at the convention. Her focus on education and her personal warmth helped humanize her husband and broaden his appeal.

- **The Shadow of the Recount:** The 2000 election ultimately came down to a razor-thin margin in Florida, leading to a highly contentious recount process. While the Republican National

Convention had successfully nominated George W. Bush and set the stage for his victory, the shadow of the recount would forever be intertwined with the legacy of the 2000 election.

The 2000 Republican National Convention, held in the heart of American history, successfully launched George W. Bush's presidential campaign. It marked a turning point for the Republican Party, embracing a more inclusive image while holding onto its core conservative values. The subsequent election, though mired in controversy, solidified the Republican Party's dominance in national politics for the first half of the new millennium.

2004: A Nation at War Rallies in the City That Never Sleeps

New York City, the epicenter of American finance, fashion, and culture, became the backdrop for a Republican National Convention unlike any other in 2004. Still reeling from the 9/11 attacks three years prior, the city bore the weight of a nation grappling with war, terrorism, and a deep sense of vulnerability. In the midst of this complex tapestry, the Republican Party sought to rally around their incumbent president, George W. Bush, and present a united front against both domestic and foreign threats.

The City and the Context: A Somber Resilience

Choosing New York City as the host for the 2004 RNC was a deliberate and symbolic act. The city, once synonymous with American optimism and ambition, had become a symbol of resilience in the face of tragedy. Hosting the convention there, just three years after the devastating attacks, served as a powerful reminder of the Bush administration's central message: strength in the face of adversity.

The city itself was a microcosm of the nation's anxieties and divisions. While the specter of 9/11 loomed large, the ongoing wars in Afghanistan and Iraq further fueled debates about national security, military intervention, and the cost of war – both human and financial. The wounds of the 2000 election, decided by a razor-thin margin in Florida, were also fresh in the minds of many Americans, further intensifying the political climate.

The Issues: War, Terrorism, and the Economy

The 2004 Republican National Convention unfolded against a backdrop of pressing issues that dominated the national conversation:

1. **The War on Terror:** The aftershocks of 9/11 continued to reverberate. The wars in Afghanistan and Iraq, launched by the Bush administration, remained deeply divisive. While Republicans argued for the necessity of these interventions, painting them as crucial battles in the war against terrorism, Democrats and a growing anti-war movement criticized their handling of the conflicts and questioned their rationale.

2. **National Security:** The threat of terrorism, particularly after 9/11, permeated the national psyche. Republicans emphasized their commitment to strengthening national security, highlighting the creation of the Department of Homeland Security and the passage of the Patriot Act as evidence of their dedication to protecting the American people.

3. The Economy: While the economy had started to recover from the recession of the early 2000s, job growth remained sluggish, and many Americans felt economically insecure. Republicans touted Bush's tax cuts as a means to stimulate economic growth, while Democrats argued that they primarily benefited the wealthy and did little to address the concerns of the middle class.

The Players: A Party United Behind Its Leader

The 2004 Republican National Convention showcased a party largely united behind its incumbent president. George W. Bush, despite facing criticism over his handling of the Iraq War and the economy, remained a popular figure among Republicans. He was flanked by prominent figures such as:

- **Dick Cheney:** Bush's Vice President, known for his hawkish foreign policy views and his influential role within the administration.
- **Rudy Giuliani:** The former Mayor of New York City, who emerged as a national hero for his leadership in the aftermath of 9/11. His powerful speech at the convention, focusing on the resilience of America and the threat of terrorism, resonated deeply with the audience.
- **Arnold Schwarzenegger:** The newly-elected Republican governor of California, a charismatic figure who embodied the party's appeal beyond its traditional base.
- **John McCain:** The Arizona Senator and former Vietnam War hero, who had challenged Bush for

the Republican nomination in 2000, crossed party lines to endorse the president, emphasizing the need for national unity in the face of terrorism.

Stories and Moments: A Tapestry of Patriotism and Protest

The 2004 RNC was not without its share of memorable moments and behind-the-scenes stories:

- **The "Security Bubble":** The convention took place under unprecedented security measures. The area surrounding Madison Square Garden, the convention venue, was heavily fortified, with thousands of police officers and National Guard troops deployed to ensure the safety of delegates and attendees.

- **The Protests:** Despite the heightened security, large-scale protests against the Iraq War and the Bush administration's policies took place throughout the city. These demonstrations, while largely peaceful, illustrated the deep divisions within American society over the war and its consequences.

- **The Clint Eastwood Factor:** Hollywood legend Clint Eastwood delivered a surprise and somewhat unconventional address at the convention, speaking directly to an empty chair representing then-presidential candidate John Kerry. The speech, while met with mixed reactions, highlighted the party's attempt to appeal to blue-collar workers and independents.

The Impact: A Pivotal Election in a Divided Nation

The 2004 Republican National Convention successfully galvanized the party base and projected an image of strength and unity in a time of national uncertainty. The carefully crafted message of leadership in the face of terrorism resonated with many Americans, ultimately contributing to President Bush's reelection victory over Democratic challenger John Kerry. The convention solidified the Republican Party's focus on national security and its appeal to a specific segment of the electorate, setting the stage for future political battles and shaping the trajectory of American politics in the 21st century.

2008: A Sea Change in St. Paul

The year 2008 marked a pivotal moment in American history. The nation reeled from the ongoing wars in Iraq and Afghanistan, economic anxieties gripped the populace, and a sense of weariness with the status quo permeated the political landscape. Against this backdrop, the Republican National Convention descended upon St. Paul, Minnesota, a city more accustomed to hosting hockey games than history-making political events.

The Setting: A Midwestern Stage

St. Paul, the "Capital City" of Minnesota, provided a unique backdrop for the 2008 RNC. Known for its charming neighborhoods, vibrant arts scene, and understated Midwestern character, the city stood in stark contrast to the high drama unfolding within the walls of the Xcel Energy Center, the convention's primary venue. The choice of St. Paul, a traditionally Democratic-leaning city in a state that hadn't voted Republican in a presidential election since 1972, was a strategic one, highlighting the party's desire to expand its appeal beyond its traditional base.

The historical context of the 2008 RNC cannot be overstated. The country grappled with the fallout from the 2008 financial crisis, triggered by a subprime mortgage meltdown that sent shockwaves through the global economy. The wars in Iraq and Afghanistan, initiated during the George W. Bush administration, continued to drain resources and test the nation's resolve. Amidst these challenges, a deep sense of uncertainty and yearning for change pervaded the American psyche.

Republican Crossroads: From Incumbent Fatigue to New Hope

Within the Republican Party, the 2008 RNC unfolded at a crossroads. The specter of George W. Bush, whose presidency had become synonymous with the Iraq War and the burgeoning economic crisis, loomed large. The party, seeking to distance itself from the unpopular incumbent while charting a new course, faced the challenge of uniting behind a candidate who could offer a compelling alternative to the burgeoning Democratic nominee, Barack Obama.

The Republican field was initially crowded, but it eventually narrowed down to two frontrunners: Senator John McCain of Arizona, a Vietnam War hero and seasoned politician, and Governor Sarah Palin of Alaska, a charismatic newcomer who electrified the conservative base. McCain, seen by many as the establishment choice, ultimately secured the nomination, selecting Palin as his running mate in a move that shook up the race and injected a dose of excitement into the Republican ticket.

The Palin Factor: Electrifying the Base, Dividing the Nation

The selection of Sarah Palin as McCain's running mate was undoubtedly the most consequential and controversial decision of the 2008 RNC. Palin, a self-described "hockey mom" and political outsider, electrified the Republican base with her conservative credentials and folksy charm. Her nomination speech, delivered with a mix of folksiness and fiery rhetoric, was a defining moment of the convention and instantly propelled her onto the national stage.

However, Palin's selection also proved deeply divisive. Critics questioned her qualifications and experience for the vice presidency, while her staunchly conservative views on social issues alienated some moderate voters. The Palin factor, while energizing the Republican base, also exposed deep fissures within the party and the nation at large.

Beyond the Headlines: Illustrious Moments and Untold Stories

Beyond the main storylines, the 2008 RNC was punctuated by a series of memorable moments and lesser-known anecdotes. Protests, a staple of any major political convention, erupted on the streets of St. Paul, with demonstrators expressing their discontent with the Bush administration's policies and the Republican Party's platform. Inside the convention hall, a sense of nervous anticipation hung in the air as delegates grappled with the weight of the moment and the uncertain future that lay ahead.

One particularly poignant moment occurred when former President George H.W. Bush, the patriarch of the Republican Party, addressed the convention in a surprise appearance. The elder Bush, while expressing support for McCain, also struck a conciliatory tone, urging unity and civility in the face of deep political divisions.

A Lasting Impact: The 2008 RNC and the Future of American Politics

The 2008 Republican National Convention left an indelible mark on American politics. The selection of Sarah Palin as McCain's running mate ushered in a new era of identity politics and cultural warfare, further polarizing the nation along partisan lines. The convention also highlighted the growing influence of the Tea Party movement, a grassroots conservative faction that would go on to play a significant role in shaping the Republican Party in the years to come.

While John McCain ultimately lost the 2008 presidential election to Barack Obama, the Republican Party emerged from the St. Paul convention energized and emboldened. The energy and enthusiasm generated by the Palin candidacy, while ultimately unsuccessful, laid the groundwork for the rise of Donald Trump and the populist wave that would sweep the party a mere eight years later.

Sunshine and Strategy: Tampa Bay, 2012

The humid air of Tampa Bay, Florida, hung thick with anticipation as the Republican National Convention descended upon the city in late August 2012. The sunshine state, known for its beaches, oranges, and often unpredictable political climate, was ready to host the GOP's quadrennial gathering, a spectacle of speeches, strategy, and the official coronation of their chosen champion to challenge President Barack Obama's bid for re-election.

The Setting and the Stakes

Tampa, a city steeped in both historical charm and modern vibrancy, provided a fitting backdrop for a party seeking to project an image of reinvention and renewal. The GOP, still smarting from their 2008 defeat, hoped that the energy of the convention, coupled with a carefully crafted message, would resonate with voters anxious about the economy and yearning for change.

The stakes couldn't have been higher. The nation, still recovering from the Great Recession, grappled with high unemployment, a sluggish housing market, and a growing national debt. These issues formed the core of the political debate, with the Republicans pinning the blame on the incumbent Democrats and offering their own vision for economic recovery.

The Protagonist and his Challenger

Mitt Romney, the former Governor of Massachusetts, had secured the Republican nomination after a bruising primary season that saw him fend off challenges from a diverse field of contenders, including the libertarian-leaning congressman Ron Paul, the social conservative Rick Santorum, and the charismatic former Speaker of the House, Newt Gingrich. Romney, with his background in business and his image as a competent manager, presented himself as the steady hand the nation needed to steer it through turbulent economic waters.

However, despite his resume and the party's unified front, Romney faced an uphill battle against the incumbent President Obama. The Democrats, skillfully leveraging the power of incumbency and Obama's enduring popularity, painted Romney as an out-of-touch elitist whose policies favored the wealthy at the expense of the middle class.

The Convention Un unfolds

The 2012 Republican National Convention, held from August 27th to 30th, played a crucial role in shaping the narrative of the election. The party faithful, gathered in the Tampa Bay Times Forum, were treated to a lineup of speakers meticulously chosen to highlight Romney's strengths and energize the base.

The convention saw fiery speeches from rising stars within the party, individuals who would go on to play significant roles in the years to come. New Jersey Governor Chris Christie delivered a rousing keynote address that electrified the crowd, while a relatively unknown congressman from Wisconsin named Paul Ryan, Romney's chosen running mate, gave a confident and articulate speech that solidified his place on the national stage.

Ann Romney, in a departure from the traditional role of a candidate's spouse, delivered a deeply personal and emotionally resonant speech. She sought to humanize her husband, presenting him not just as a successful businessman but as a loving husband and father. Her speech aimed to soften Romney's image and make him more relatable to undecided voters.

The "We Built This" Controversy

The convention wasn't without its share of controversy. Clint Eastwood, the legendary actor, delivered an offbeat and unscripted address to an empty chair representing President Obama. While intended as humorous, the segment fell flat with many viewers and became fodder for late-night talk show hosts.

A more substantial controversy arose from Romney's own words. During a campaign stop, he uttered the phrase "We built this," referring to successful businesses, which was quickly seized upon by the Democrats and spun as evidence of Romney's disconnect from the struggles of ordinary Americans.

This gaffe, amplified by the media, dogged Romney throughout the remainder of the campaign.

The Legacy of Tampa Bay

The 2012 Republican National Convention achieved its primary objective of formally nominating Mitt Romney and introducing his running mate, Paul Ryan. The carefully choreographed event showcased the party's platform, energized its base, and attempted to reframe Romney's image for the general electorate.

However, despite the convention's energy and the party's best efforts, Romney ultimately lost the election to Barack Obama. The Democrats' superior ground game, coupled with their effective messaging and fundraising, proved insurmountable.

The 2012 RNC, despite its outcome, holds a unique place in the annals of American political history. It marked the rise of future political stars, exposed deep divisions within the electorate, and provided a glimpse into the evolving strategies of a party grappling with its identity in a rapidly changing political landscape. The echoes of Tampa Bay, from its soaring rhetoric to its missteps, continue to resonate within the Republican Party, shaping its trajectory and influencing its approach to future elections.

Cleveland 2016 - A Crown of Thorns

The City of Rock and Roll Meets the Grand Old Party

The 2016 Republican National Convention, held from July 18th to 21st, chose Cleveland, Ohio, as its battleground. This was a calculated move. Ohio, a perennial swing state, held symbolic importance. The GOP, eager to recapture the White House after eight years, saw an opportunity to court the Rust Belt, a region hit hard by economic anxieties. Cleveland itself, once a symbol of industrial might, was experiencing a rebirth. Hosting the RNC was a chance to showcase this transformation.

A Nation Divided, A Party in Flux

The year 2016 was a pressure cooker of political and social tension. The country grappled with issues of racial injustice, economic inequality, and terrorism. The rise of social media amplified these anxieties, creating echo chambers and deepening existing divides. Within the Republican Party, the Tea Party movement, which had gained traction since 2009, continued to push the party rightward, challenging the establishment and demanding a more populist, anti-establishment agenda.

This internal conflict played out dramatically in the Republican primaries. The party found itself with an unprecedented 17 candidates, a mix of establishment figures, Tea Party favorites, and political outsiders. The eventual nominee, Donald J. Trump, was unlike any other in American history. A real estate mogul and reality TV star with no prior political experience, Trump tapped into the simmering anger and frustration felt by many Americans, particularly white, working-class voters who felt left behind by globalization and societal changes.

The Leaders on the Stage, the Rumblings Offstage

The convention itself reflected the tumultuous state of the party. Reince Priebus, the RNC chairman, faced the unenviable task of uniting a fractured party behind a controversial nominee. Trump, known for his brash style and unconventional campaign, dominated the news cycle. His running mate, Indiana Governor Mike Pence, a staunch social conservative, was chosen to balance the ticket and appeal to the party's base.

The convention saw a parade of speakers, each aiming to present a united front and make the case for a Trump presidency. Notable figures included members of the Trump family, such as Melania Trump, whose speech was later overshadowed by plagiarism accusations, and Donald Trump Jr., who delivered a fiery address attacking Hillary Clinton, the Democratic nominee. Other speakers included prominent Republicans like Ted Cruz, Marco Rubio, and Paul Ryan, some of whom had clashed fiercely with Trump during the primaries.

"Make America Great Again" and the Echoes of Change

The 2016 RNC will be remembered for several key moments. First, it solidified the Republican Party's shift towards populism and nationalism. Trump's acceptance speech, delivered against a backdrop of "Make America Great Again" signs, hammered home his message of economic nationalism, tough immigration policies, and a return to "law and order." This resonated with a segment of the electorate who felt unheard by the political establishment and yearned for a return to a perceived better time.

Second, the convention highlighted the deep divisions within the party. Ted Cruz's refusal to endorse Trump during his speech, a highly unusual move for a former primary opponent, exposed the rift between the party's establishment and its more populist wing. This internal struggle continues to shape the Republican Party's identity and direction.

Lastly, the 2016 RNC foreshadowed the increasingly polarized and bitter political climate that has come to define American politics. The convention saw protests and counter-protests, highlighting the deep societal divisions over race, immigration, and social issues. The tone of the convention, often described as dark and divisive, set the stage for a bruising general election campaign.

The Legacy: A Turning Point in American Politics

The 2016 Republican National Convention was more than just a political event; it was a cultural moment that revealed the anxieties, frustrations, and divisions within American society. It marked a turning point for the Republican Party, pushing it further rightward and solidifying its embrace of populism. The convention, and the election that followed, have had a profound and lasting impact on American politics, leaving the country grappling with its legacy for years to come.

2020: A Convention Unlike Any Other

The 2020 Republican National Convention, initially slated for Charlotte, North Carolina, was dramatically reshaped by the convergence of a global pandemic and a nation grappling with social unrest. Ultimately a hybrid event, with some events in Charlotte and others in Washington D.C., the convention served less as a traditional nomination celebration and more as a platform to solidify President Donald Trump's image as a strong leader amidst chaos.

A Nation Divided, A Party Redefined

The backdrop for the 2020 RNC was anything but ordinary. The COVID-19 pandemic had gripped the nation, forcing lockdowns and upending daily life. The death of George Floyd at the hands of police in May 2020 ignited protests against racial injustice and police brutality across the country, further highlighting existing societal divisions.

Within this turbulent context, the Republican party, under President Trump's leadership, had undergone a significant transformation. Traditional conservative values were increasingly intertwined with populist rhetoric and a rejection of established norms. The party's platform focused heavily on themes of "law and order," economic nationalism, and a staunch defense of what they deemed "American values."

Charlotte and Beyond: The Shifting Stage

Initially, Charlotte, North Carolina was chosen to host the 2020 RNC. However, disputes arose between the city and the Republican National Committee (RNC) over COVID-19 safety protocols, particularly regarding mask mandates and social distancing requirements that the RNC was unwilling to implement.

This disagreement led to a highly unusual move: in June 2020, President Trump announced that the Republican National Convention would be moved from Charlotte. While some official business remained in Charlotte, the majority of the convention, including Trump's acceptance speech, would be held in Washington D.C. This shift, a stark break from tradition, highlighted the growing tension between the Republican party's vision and the realities of the pandemic.

Faces of the Party: Leaders and Loyalists

The 2020 RNC showcased a Republican party firmly aligned with President Trump. Vice President Mike Pence remained a steadfast presence, while figures like Donald Trump Jr., Ivanka Trump, and Lara Trump played prominent roles in amplifying the president's message.

Notable speeches came from individuals like Nikki Haley, then former U.S. Ambassador to the United

Nations, who sought to broaden the party's appeal beyond Trump's base, and Senator Tim Scott, who delivered a powerful address about his experiences with racism and his belief in the American dream.

Beyond the Podium: Lasting Images and Echoes

The 2020 RNC was notable for its unconventional format and its stark departure from the celebratory atmosphere of past conventions. Held against a backdrop of national unrest and a raging pandemic, the event primarily functioned as a platform for President Trump to solidify his base and project an image of strength and leadership.

Several moments from the convention remain etched in public memory. Perhaps the most controversial was President Trump's acceptance speech delivered from the South Lawn of the White House, a move widely criticized for blurring the lines between campaigning and official government business. Other notable moments included the diverse range of speakers, many of whom shared personal stories aimed at humanizing the President's policies.

A Legacy of Division and Uncertainty

The 2020 Republican National Convention reflected the turbulent times in which it occurred. The ongoing pandemic, the protests for racial justice, and the deeply polarized political climate cast a long shadow over the event. While the convention served its primary purpose of renominating Donald Trump for president, it did little to bridge the divides within the nation. Instead, it further solidified the Republican party's transformation under Trump, emphasizing a message of cultural conservatism, economic populism, and a strongman image for its leader. The long-term impact of the 2020 RNC on American history is still unfolding, but it undoubtedly stands as a stark reminder of the political and social fissures that continue to shape the nation's trajectory.